THE
SOUTHERN
SYMPATHY
COOKBOOK

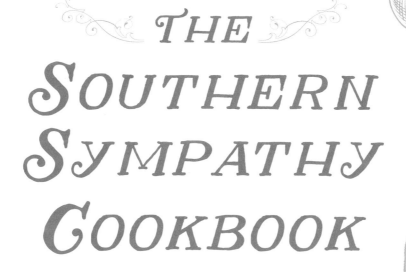

THE
SOUTHERN
SYMPATHY
COOKBOOK

Funeral Food with a Twist

PERRE COLEMAN MAGNESS

The Countryman Press
A division of W. W. Norton & Company
Independent Publishers Since 1923

Manufacturing by Versa Press
Book design by Faceout Studio
Production manager: Devon Zahn

The Countryman Press
www.countrymanpress.com

A division of W. W. Norton & Company
500 Fifth Avenue, New York, NY 10110
www.wwnorton.com

978-1-68268-038-4

3 4 5 6 7 8 9 0

When we all have food to eat
When we all have food to eat
O Lord, I want to be in that number
When the Saints go marching in
—"When The Saints Go Marching In"

CONTENTS

INTRODUCTION

Nothing motivates one to get in the kitchen more than a funeral. We all seem to harbor that primordial need to comfort with food.

Funerals in the South are synonymous with food. Even if it's a hastily thrown together deli tray, a jar of homemade dressing and a bag of salad greens, or a pound cake from the freezer, the first thought is "How can I feed them?" Small town communities, urban social circles and religious congregations can pull together a plan with a rapidity and precision world military leaders can envy. Phone trees, sign-up sheets, and now email blasts and text chains organize everything a grieving family could need. The table at any visitation, celebration of life, or home-going is like an encyclopedia of local foodways, or a precise study in the cultural anthropology of a society. We often express our emotions and process our grief through the act of nourishing our neighbors. Southern author and humorist Julia Reed perhaps puts it most succinctly. She tells the story of her grandparents, unexpected death in an accident. The dreaded call came and her mother leapt into action to make all the necessary arrangements. Knowing what was to come, as she rushed out of the house, she gave Julia one instruction: "Go clean out the refrigerator."

There are times when your instinct, your heart's reaction, is to prepare food. Comforting, sustaining, and, well, practical food.

"Neighbors bring food with death and flowers with sickness and little things in between."

—Harper Lee, *To Kill a Mockingbird*

To comfort a grieving family and remove at least one mundane worry. To help out a friend in need who would do, or has done, the same for you. To feel useful in a fearful time. The problem is, what exactly to make. Too often we, and everyone around us, turn to standards—recipes we see as foolproof, know how to make on short notice, know they reheat and keep well. Recipes that we keep in mind, or maybe on a card at the front of the recipe box for easy access. A hearty, comforting dish that we know how to make and how to make well, that we can whip up the instant the call comes. What we really want to do, intend to do, is to deliver a dish that is wholesome, satisfying and, most of all, enjoyable. Something that will be truly appreciated and do what we mean it to—provide comfort, show kindness and hopefully bring some joy.

The recipes in this book are meant to do just that—dishes perfect for the funeral gathering, or for a bereaved family at home. Whether it's a full-on casserole, a traditional molded salad, or a simple breakfast or snack, I've included recipes that cover all the bases. But of course, you don't have to wait for a funeral to try any of them out.

The Great Awakening

BREAKFAST AND BREAD

SWEET TEA BREAD

Sweet Tea is so ubiquitous and all encompassing in the South, we use it in just about any way we can. This light, delicately flavored quick bread is perfect for breakfast or an afternoon gathering, packaged up nicely with a ribbon or sliced on a silver platter.

:: MAKES 1 LOAF

Put the tea bag and 2 sprigs of mint in a measuring cup. Add 1 cup boiling water. Steep for 30 minutes, then remove the tea bag and mint. Cool to room temperature.

Preheat the oven to 350°F. Spray a 9-by-5-inch loaf pan with baking spray.

Beat the butter and sugar together in the bowl of a stand mixer fitted with the paddle attachment until light and fluffy. Beat in the lemon zest and 1 tablespoon of finely chopped fresh mint. Add the eggs, one at a time, beating well after each addition and scraping down the sides of the bowl.

Measure out ½ cup of the tea, reserving the rest for the glaze. Add the flour, baking powder and salt to the butter in the bowl in three additions, alternating with the tea and scraping down the sides of the bowl. When everything is well combined, beat on high for 5 seconds, then scrape the batter into the prepared pan and smooth into an even layer.

Bake for 45 to 50 minutes until a tester inserted in the center comes out clean. Cool in the pan for 10 minutes, then remove to a wire rack to cool completely. Meanwhile, prepare the glaze.

Sift the confectioners' sugar into a small bowl. Whisk in the remaining tea slowly, until you have a pourable glaze about the consistency of heavy cream. Drizzle the glaze over the cake with a spoon, spreading to cover the top with a few attractive drips down the sides. Let the glaze set for about an hour.

The loaf will keep in an airtight container for a day.

1 family-sized tea bag

2 sprigs mint, plus 1 tablespoon finely chopped mint

8 tablespoons (1 stick) unsalted butter, at room temperature

¾ cup granulated sugar

Zest of one medium lemon

2 large eggs

1½ cups all-purpose flour

½ teaspoon baking powder

½ teaspoon salt

¾ cup confectioners' sugar

The Visitation

Many Southern funerals include the visitation. That may sound like the spectral appearance of our departed loved one, but no. The visitation is the reception, frequently the day before or immediately after the funeral. It's a chance for everyone to talk to the bereaved, share memories of the deceased, and really get their feed on. And, equally important, for the ladies in the equation to show off their skills in the kitchen. Friends and family of the recently departed are in the kitchen, bustling around in their funeral best, maybe with an apron thrown on top, looking for serving pieces and Saran Wrap, deciding what goes on the table and what goes in the fridge for later. In many small towns, the visitation is held in a church hall, with the ladies of the church supplying much of the food. In other places, the visitation takes place at the funeral home or the home of the deceased, with friends supplying the buffet.

BUTTERMILK BANANA BREAD

Banana bread is almost a talisman—everyone seems to have a recipe they can whip up without a thought, and it's a food gift people always appreciate. I decided I should create a recipe that meets my banana bread tastes. I started with buttermilk, because I adore using buttermilk for baking. It keeps the bread moist and adds a nice little tang. I find it highlights the fresh banana taste. I left out the extras—I like nuts, but not always in baked goods, and again, I want a banana bread that tastes like bananas. So this is my house banana bread. Simple and straightforward, with lots of banana flavor.

:: **MAKES 1 LOAF**

8 tablespoons (1 stick) unsalted butter, softened

1 cup granulated sugar

2 eggs

1 teaspoon baking soda

½ cup buttermilk

1 teaspoon baking powder

2 cups all-purpose flour

1 cup mashed ripe banana (about 3 bananas)

Grease a 9-by-5-inch loaf pan. Preheat the oven to 350°F.

Beat the butter and sugar together in the bowl of a stand mixer fitted with the paddle attachment until light and fluffy. Add the eggs, one at a time, beating well after each addition. Mix the baking soda into the buttermilk and add the baking powder to the flour. Beat the flour and the buttermilk alternately into the butter, scraping the sides of the bowl a few times, until thoroughly combined. Beat in the mashed bananas.

Scrape the batter into the prepared pan and bake for 1 to 1¼ hours until a tester inserted in the center comes out with just a few damp crumbs clinging to it. If the top begins to brown too deeply, loosely cover the top with foil.

Cool in the pan for a few minutes, then turn out onto a wire rack to cool completely.

"She had no hobbies, made no contribution to society and rarely shared a kind word or deed in her life. I speak for the majority of her family when I say her presence will not be missed by many, very few tears will be shed and there will be no lamenting over her passing."

—*Obituary, Galveston, Texas*

FRESH STRAWBERRY BREAD

I remember a delicious quick bread popular when I was kid, sweet and cinnamony with nice pockets of gooey strawberry. I think I even remember making it myself at some point. So I went looking for recipes, and they all contained frozen berries in syrup—some even used cake mix or pudding mix. But I thought surely I could do better than that. Fresh, in-season, local strawberries are one of life's great pleasures, so why muck them up with chemicals and additives and fake gunk. Here is my new result—sweet, fresh, spiced bread perfect for breakfast, or tea, or even dessert.

:: MAKES 1 LOAF

Slice the strawberries and place in a bowl. Sprinkle over the 3 tablespoons of sugar and toss to thoroughly coat the berries. Leave to macerate for several hours, until there is plenty of juice at the bottom of the bowl. Drain the berries, reserving the juice.

Preheat the oven to 350°F. Grease a 9-by-5-inch loaf pan.

Mix the flour, remaining 1 cup sugar, baking soda, salt, and cinnamon in a large bowl. Add the eggs, vegetable oil, and vanilla and mix until just combined. Fold in the drained strawberry slices, distributing evenly. Pour the batter into the prepared loaf pan and bake for 45 minutes to an hour, until a tester inserted in the middle of the loaf comes out clean.

Remove the loaf from the oven and poke holes all over the top with a skewer or thin knife. Drizzle about ¼ cup of reserved strawberry juice over the top of the bread, allowing it to soak in. Loosen the cake from the sides of the pan with a thin knife and leave to cool in the pan.

10 ounces fresh strawberries, stemmed and sliced

1 cup plus 3 tablespoons granulated sugar

1½ cups all-purpose flour

½ teaspoon baking soda

½ teaspoon salt

½ teaspoon ground cinnamon

2 eggs

½ cup vegetable oil

½ teaspoon vanilla extract

HUMMINGBIRD MUFFINS WITH PINEAPPLE GLAZE

Hummingbird cake is a Southern classic of the complex, towering layered variety. But the ingredients of bananas, pineapples, and coconut lend themselves so beautifully to a breakfast iteration that I couldn't resist turning this cake table favorite into a morning treat (that's also a perfect afternoon snack). The muffins are packed with flavor and the glaze adds a hit of sweetness that harks to the original's fluffy frosting, without nearly as much work.

:: MAKES 12

Preheat the oven to 350°F. Spray 12 muffin cups with baking spray, or line with paper liners.

Drain the pineapple in a colander into a small bowl, reserving the juice.

Place the flour, sugar, baking powder, and nutmeg in a large mixing bowl and stir with a fork to combine. Crumble in the coconut, breaking up any large clumps with your fingers. Add the pecans and stir to distribute everything evenly. Stir the pineapple, banana, oil, orange zest, 1 tablespoon orange juice, and vanilla together in a medium bowl until well combined. Add the eggs and stir with a fork until all the ingredients are combined and creamy.

Pour the wet ingredients into the dry and fold together until just combined, with no visible dry ingredients in the batter or the bowl.

Divide the batter between the muffin cups and bake for 15 to 18 minutes, until a tester inserted in the center of a muffin comes out clean. Cool in the pan for 20 minutes, then remove to a wire rack set over waxed paper or foil to catch drips from the glaze to make cleanup easy. Cool completely.

1 (8-ounce) can crushed pineapple

2 cups all-purpose flour

1 cup granulated sugar

1½ teaspoons baking powder

¼ teaspoon nutmeg

½ cup sweetened shredded coconut

½ cup chopped pecans

1 cup mashed banana (from 2 large bananas)

¾ cup canola oil

Zest and juice of one small navel orange

1 teaspoon vanilla

2 eggs

1 cup confectioners' sugar

Catherine

Catherine had only been
married for a few weeks
when her husband's
grandfather passed.
At the visitation at
the funeral home, she
encountered her first open
casket, and was surprised
to find all the family
gathered around examining
and commenting on the
deceased's suit and tie and
general ensemble. Catherine,
trying to be helpful to her
new family, asked if there was
anything she could do to help.
She was quickly dispatched
back to the house to find
his glasses, because
according to the family,
"he just didn't look right."

Sift the confectioners' sugar into a small bowl and whisk in 1 tablespoon of the reserved pineapple juice and 1 tablespoon of the reserved orange juice until smooth and creamy. Dip the top of each muffin into the glaze, turning it around to cover the whole top, then lift it out and let any excess glaze drip off. Return the muffin right-side up to the cooling rack and repeat with the remaining muffins. Leave for about 30 minutes for the glaze to set.

Note: The muffins will keep in an airtight container for a day. They will last for 3 days without the glaze.

PECAN BITES

I've been making this recipe, or a version of it, for as long as I can remember. It is another community cookbook classic. These rich little bites are a perfect pickup breakfast and pair beautifully with a fruit bowl or Ambrosia with Rosemary and Honey Syrup (page 82). They even make for a nice change in a dinnertime bread basket.

:: MAKES 24

Preheat the oven to 350°F. Spray 24 mini-muffin cups with baking spray.

Stir the melted butter, eggs, and brown sugar together in a medium mixing bowl until thoroughly combined. Stir in the flour and vanilla to combine, then fold in the nuts to evenly distribute.

Divide the batter equally in the muffin cups, topping each with a pecan half, if using. Bake for 20 minutes until golden and firm.

8 tablespoons (1 stick) unsalted butter, melted and cooled

2 eggs

1 cup dark brown sugar

½ cup all-purpose flour

1 teaspoon vanilla

1½ cups chopped pecans, plus additional pecan halves, for garnish (optional)

"Heaven now smiles with the addition of this precious soul from our midst whose radiant spirit shall now join with the elders, the angels, the saints and the heavenly chorus in singing praises unto God throughout the eternal ages."

—Obituary, Memphis, Tennessee

CINNAMON BISCUIT BITES

Dedicated biscuit makers have long employed the trick of rolling the scraps from cutting biscuits in butter and cinnamon sugar and baking them separately to snack on before the biscuits are served. I take that a step further with a from-scratch cinnamon biscuit dish. It's the glaze that makes these sweet; the biscuits are simply packed with cinnamon flavor.

:: MAKES ABOUT 14 BISCUITS

Pour the melted butter into a 10-inch pie plate and swirl to cover the bottom of the dish. In a small bowl, mix the granulated and brown sugars, cinnamon, and nutmeg together with a fork, breaking up any lumps of brown sugar.

Mix the flour, baking powder, and salt together in a medium mixing bowl. Cut the cold butter into very small pieces and drop in the bowl. Toss the butter around with a fork or your good, clean fingers to coat with the flour. Use a pastry blender or fork to rub the butter and flour together until you have a crumbly mixture with a few larger pieces of butter visible. Add the buttermilk ¼ cup at a time until the dough comes together in a soft ball of dough. You may not use all the buttermilk. Pinch off pieces of the dough and roll into balls about the size of a golf ball. Roll each ball in the cinnamon-sugar mixture, then place it in the prepared pie plate.

At this point, the pan can be covered and refrigerated overnight. When ready to bake, preheat the oven to 350°F. Bake the biscuits for 25 minutes until cooked through and firm. Let cool for about 10 minutes. Beat the confectioners' sugar with enough milk to make a pourable glaze, about the consistency of heavy cream. Drizzle the glaze over the biscuits and leave for a few minutes to set. Leftover biscuit bites can be cooled and covered for a day.

4 tablespoons (½ stick) unsalted butter, melted, plus 8 tablespoons (1 stick), cold

¼ cup granulated sugar

¼ cup light brown sugar

1 tablespoon cinnamon

¼ teaspoon nutmeg

2 cups soft wheat flour (such as White Lily)

1 tablespoon baking powder

½ teaspoon kosher salt

¾ to 1 cup buttermilk

⅓ cup confectioners' sugar

1 to 2 tablespoons milk

SOUTHERN SWEET POTATO CRUMB CAKE

I am a latecomer to the joys of sweet potato, but now I can't get enough of the earthy, nutty flavor. I once assumed they existed only in the context of Thanksgiving, and somehow came out of the ground covered in marshmallows. But the versatility of the sweet potato is one of its greatest gifts. Rich, moist, sweet cake tinged orange from the sweet potatoes and loaded with a buttery, crumbly topping takes breakfast to a whole new level.

:: SERVES 12

FOR THE CRUMBLE:

Whisk the flour, brown sugar, spices, and salt together in a large bowl, breaking up any lumps of sugar. Pour in the melted butter and stir to combine. Use your good, clean hands to finish blending, creating a lovely spiced rubble. Set aside.

FOR THE CAKE:

Prick the potatoes all over with a sharp knife and microwave for 10 minutes until soft when pressed. When the potatoes are cool enough to handle, but still warm, cut in half and scoop the flesh into the bowl of a food processor. Process until you have a smooth puree, scraping down the sides of the bowl as needed. You should have about a cup of puree (measure to be sure, save any extra for another use). Leave the puree to cool.

Preheat the oven to 350°F. Spray a 9-by-13-by-2-inch baking pan with nonstick baking spray.

Mix the flour, sugar, baking powder, nutmeg, and salt together in a very large mixing bowl. Make sure everything is evenly distributed. To the sweet potato puree in the food processor, add the eggs, buttermilk, oil, sorghum, and vanilla and blend until smooth. Scrape all the wet ingredients into the dry and mix just until combined and there are no dry ingredients visible in the bowl. The batter will be thick.

For the Crumble:

3 cups all-purpose flour

1½ cups light brown sugar

1 tablespoon ground cinnamon

1 teaspoon ground nutmeg

½ teaspoon kosher salt

20 tablespoons (2½ sticks) unsalted butter, melted

For the Cake:

2 medium sweet potatoes

3 cups all-purpose flour

1 cup granulated sugar

1 tablespoon baking powder

1 teaspoon ground nutmeg

½ teaspoon kosher salt

2 large eggs

1 cup whole buttermilk

¼ cup vegetable oil

¼ cup sorghum syrup

1 tablespoon vanilla extract

Spread the batter into the prepared pan, and use slightly damp, clean hands to press it into an even layer, all the way to the corners. Use your clean, dry hands to crumble the crumb topping in an even layer all over the batter, again making sure to cover the corners and edges of the cake. Break up any large lumps as you go. Lightly press the crumble into the batter.

Bake the cake for 40 to 45 minutes, until a tester inserted in the center comes out clean. Cool in the pan.

"I did not attend his funeral, but I sent a nice letter saying I approved of it."

—Mark Twain

PEACHES AND CREAM COFFEE CAKE

Sweet Southern peaches are one of the true joys of summer, nothing like the dry and mealy all-year-round version sold in grocery stores in any season. So for the sweet flavor of peaches off-season, I turn to preserves, made by me or a local purveyor, or from a good Southern brand. This coffee cake is sweet and rich with a delightful creamy filling and a beautiful ribbon of peach.

:: SERVES 12

FOR THE CAKE:

Preheat the oven to 350°F. Spray an 8-inch square baking pan with baking spray.

Mix the flour, sugar, and cinnamon together in the bowl of a stand mixer. Cut the butter into small pieces and sprinkle over the flour in the bowl. Beat on medium speed until the butter is well mixed with the dry ingredients and resembles rough crumbs. You can use your hands to rub any large clumps of butter into the flour. Scoop out 1 cup of the mixture for the crumb topping. Add the baking powder, baking soda, and salt to the remaining mix and blend to combine. Add the buttermilk, egg, and vanilla, and beat until the mixture is smooth and completely combined. Scrape the batter into the prepared pan and spread it out into an even layer. Use slightly dampened fingers to press the batter to the edges of the pan, pressing so some batter pushes up the sides of the pan and there is an indentation for the filling with about a ¼-inch border.

FOR THE FILLING:

Clean out the mixer bowl, then beat the cream cheese, egg, sugar, and vanilla together until smooth. Spread the cream cheese over the batter, filling the indention, to about ¼ inch from the edge of the batter. Dollop the peach preserves over the filling with a spoon, then use the back of the spoon to spread them out to an

For the Cake:

2¼ cups all-purpose flour

¾ cup granulated sugar

1 teaspoon cinnamon

12 tablespoons (1½ sticks) unsalted butter, cold

½ teaspoon baking powder

½ teaspoon baking soda

½ teaspoon kosher salt

1 cup buttermilk

1 large egg

1 teaspoon vanilla extract

For the Filling:

1 (8-ounce) package cream cheese, softened

1 large egg

¼ cup granulated sugar

1 teaspoon vanilla extract

1 cup peach preserves (such as Braswell's)

even layer. Sprinkle the reserved crumbs in an even layer over the preserves.

Bake the coffee cake for 45 minutes, until a tester inserted in the center comes out clean. The center may still be a little wobbly—trust the tester.

Cool completely and serve in small squares. The cake will keep, covered tightly, for a day.

COUNTRY SAUSAGE BALLS

Sausage balls—made with baking mix, sausage, and cheese—are a favorite childhood memory for me. In fact, when I was away in college and grad school, I'd always ask my mom to make these for me when I came home. Most everyone I know has made sausage balls at some point in their life. And they are the perfect take-along treat. They can be eaten for breakfast, as a snack, or with cocktails. They can be delivered frozen and ready to bake or fully cooked; and you can keep a batch in the freezer for last-minute needs. This version will appeal to the Southern culinary classicist and new discoverers. I've switched out the baking mix and added a little cornmeal for texture and some fresh herbs for flavor to create a new and exciting sausage ball experience.

:: **MAKES ABOUT 30 BALLS**

1¾ cups all-purpose flour

¼ cup coarse yellow cornmeal

2 teaspoons very finely chopped fresh rosemary

1 teaspoon baking powder

1 teaspoon kosher salt

½ teaspoon ground black pepper

2 tablespoons unsalted butter, cold

1 pound breakfast sausage, at room temperature

8 ounces sharp Cheddar (I like to use white Cheddar, but yellow works as well), finely grated

2 to 4 tablespoons whole milk

Whisk the flour, cornmeal, rosemary, baking powder, salt, and pepper together in the bowl of a stand mixer. Cut the butter into small pieces and drop them into the flour, then with the paddle attachment, beat until the butter is broken up into the dry ingredients. Add the sausage and cheese and 2 tablespoons of the milk, and beat until everything is well and evenly combined. You may add a little more milk as needed to make it all come together in a ball.

Roll the dough into golf-ball-sized balls and place ½ inch apart on the prepared baking sheet. Bake for 15 to 20 minutes, until the balls are golden brown and cooked through.

The uncooked balls can be placed on a waxed paper–lined tray and frozen until hard. Transfer to a zip-top plastic bag and keep in the freezer for 3 months. If cooking from frozen, increase the cooking time by about 10 minutes.

"[Her first] marriage . . . was a three-ring circus: engagement ring, wedding ring, and suffering. . . . 'I never knew what happiness was until I remarried, and by then it was too late' . . . [She] slipped away and joined her daughter in Heaven. Fortunately, [her husband] preceded her and joined his mother in a much warmer climate."

—*Obituary, Memphis, Tennessee*

BISCUITS AND GRAVY BREAKFAST BAKE

Biscuits and gravy is my all time favorite breakfast. I make it for myself as a special treat and order it at fancy Southern brunch restaurants, mom and pop diners, and fast food joints. This casserole gives you all the flavor of biscuits and gravy in a make-ahead dish that conveniently also includes eggs for a complete breakfast experience.

:: SERVES 10

FOR THE GRAVY:

Crumble the sausage into a large skillet and cook over medium-high heat until browned and no longer pink in the center. Break the sausage into very small pieces as it cooks. When the sausage is done, remove it to a paper towel–lined plate to drain. There should be no more than 1 tablespoon fat left in the pan; drain off any excess. Drop the green onions into the fat in the pan and cook, stirring frequently, until soft and wilted. Add the butter and when it is melted, sprinkle over the flour and stir to combine. It will make a thick paste. Whisk in the milk and bring to a bubble, whisking frequently to smooth it out. Add the sage, salt, and pepper. Cook until thick and smooth, then remove from the heat and stir the sausage back into the gravy. Set aside to cool.

FOR THE BISCUIT BASE:

Whisk the flour, baking powder, and salt together in a medium mixing bowl. Cut the butter into small pieces and rub it into the flour with a pastry blender or fork until you have a crumbly mixture with a few larger lumps of butter visible. Add the milk, a little at a time, stirring together, until you have a dough of a soft, dropping consistency. You may not use all the milk. Stir together until all the dry ingredients are incorporated, then drop spoonfuls of the dough over the bottom of a greased 9-by-13-inch

For the Gravy:

1 pound ground breakfast sausage

4 green onions, white and light green parts, finely chopped

2 tablespoons unsalted butter

¼ cup all-purpose flour

2 cups whole milk

1 tablespoon chopped fresh sage

1 teaspoon kosher salt

1 teaspoon ground black pepper

For the Biscuit Base:

2 cups all-purpose flour

3 teaspoons baking powder

½ teaspoon kosher salt

2 tablespoons unsalted butter, cold

¾ to 1 cup whole milk

2 cups grated sharp Cheddar

6 eggs

¼ cup whole milk

1 tablespoon chopped fresh sage

1 teaspoon hot sauce

1 teaspoon kosher salt

½ teaspoon ground black pepper

baking pan. Use lightly dampened fingers to press the biscuit dough into a flat layer—you are not trying to completely cover the bottom of the dish, just distribute the biscuit dough evenly.

FOR THE FILLING:

Evenly sprinkle half of the grated cheddar over the biscuit dough. Wipe out the mixing bowl, then beat the eggs, milk, sage, hot sauce, salt, and pepper together until thoroughly blended. Pour over the biscuit base and tilt the pan to distribute the eggs over the top of the biscuit dough.

Dollop spoonfuls of the cooled sausage gravy over the top of the eggs, again working to evenly distribute the gravy and sausage over the casserole rather than cover the previous layers. Sprinkle the remaining cheese evenly over the casserole.

At this point, the casserole can be covered and refrigerated for up to 12 hours. When ready to bake, remove the dish from the fridge while the oven preheats to 350°F. Bake for 40 to 45 minutes until heated through, browned, and bubbly. Serve hot.

ANGEL BISCUITS

There is nothing so Southern and so comforting as home-baked biscuits. And in the context of funeral food, I think it only appropriate to make them angel biscuits. Yeast added to a typical butter-milk biscuit recipe makes them rise up to the heavens, as light as angel wings.

:: MAKES ABOUT 24 BISCUITS

Preheat the oven to 400°F. Line a rimmed baking sheet with parchment paper.

Stir the yeast into the warm water in a small measuring jug and leave to sit for 5 minutes until bubbly.

Whisk the flour, sugar, baking powder, baking soda, and salt together in a large mixing bowl. Cut the butter and the short-ening into small cubes and sprinkle over the flour in the bowl. Use a fork to toss the cubes lightly in the flour to coat. Then dip your clean fingers into some flour and mix everything together, squishing and rubbing the mixture to combine the fats and the flour. Don't spend too long doing this, gentle handling is the key to a tender biscuit. It's all right if there are some lumps of butter or shortening left. Many recipes describe the result of this process as looking like breadcrumbs or fine meal, and that's okay. I think it looks like lumpy flour. When you pinch a bit of flour between your fingers, from anywhere in the bowl, it should stick together.

Mix the buttermilk and yeasty water together, then pour this over the flour. Use the fork to fold the buttermilk into the dough, carefully incorporating the liquid. Again, you don't want to work the dough too much, but don't leave much loose, dry flour in the bottom of the bowl. You can use your hands to get that last bit of dry flour into the dough.

Lightly flour a work surface. I find the counter top to be best; a board tends to slip around. You do want to use a light hand to flour the surface, because too much will leave an unpleasant floury coating on the biscuits. Sprinkling flour through a wire sieve is a great way to do this.

Turn the dough out onto the surface, and turn it over on itself once or twice to bring the dough together. I do not say knead, because you don't want to work the dough that hard. Press the

1 (¼-ounce) package active dry yeast

¼ cup warm water (about 110°F)

5 cups soft wheat flour (such as White Lily)

2 tablespoons granulated sugar

1 teaspoon baking powder

1 teaspoon baking soda

1 teaspoon salt

8 tablespoons (1 stick) unsalted butter, cold

½ cup vegetable shortening

1½ cups whole buttermilk

dough into a rectangle about ½-inch thick. Just press it out lightly with your hands to an even thickness. This method makes the top of the biscuits slightly textured, which looks very homemade, but if it bothers you, roll a lightly floured rolling pin lightly over the top.

Cut the biscuits with a round cutter, always cutting as close to the edge of the dough and as close together as you can to get as many biscuits as possible. Just press the cutter down and pull back up; don't twist or the sides won't rise up as nicely. You can also cut the biscuits into 2-inch squares, in which case you won't have scraps of dough left over. Place the biscuits very close to each other on the prepared pan, just touching.

Cook the biscuits for 12 to 15 minutes, just until they are risen and lightly golden.

You can roll and cut out the biscuits, place them on the baking sheet, and freeze until hard, about 2 hours. Transfer them to a zip-top plastic bag and store in the freezer for up to a month. To bake, remove from the freezer, place on a baking sheet and let stand for 30 minutes, then proceed as above.

SIMPLE BUTTERMILK YEAST ROLLS

I have dreamed most of my life of being a person who makes beautiful, old-fashioned dinner rolls. Alas, I am not and like many Southerners these days, I buy them in little tin pans. But I know I must have at least one homemade roll recipe under my belt, and I chose this one, which is foolproof even for the most yeast averse and does not require a huge time commitment. And I promise, people will swoon over your homemade rolls—as much for the flavor as for the fact you made them yourself. Use instant dried yeast that comes in a jar rather than active yeast from packets.

:: **MAKES 12 ROLLS**

Preheat oven to 400°F. Lightly grease a 9-by-13-inch rimmed sheet pan.

Melt the 4 tablespoons butter in a small saucepan over low heat, then add the buttermilk and heat until it reaches 110°F, just barely bubbling.

Place the yeast and the honey in the bowl of a stand mixer fitted with the paddle attachment and mix until just combined. Add the buttermilk and butter when it comes to temperature and blend. With the motor running, add the egg and the salt and beat until combined, then beat in the flour ½ cup at a time until the dough clings to the beater in a sticky ball. You may not need all the flour.

With lightly floured hands, pull the dough from the beater, roll it into 12 balls, and place these on the prepared baking sheet. Cover the sheet with a tea towel and leave the rolls to rise for 10 minutes.

Bake for 8 to 12 minutes, until they are golden and cooked through.

Brush the top of the rolls with 2 tablespoons melted butter.

4 tablespoons (½ stick) unsalted butter, plus 2 tablespoons, melted

1 cup buttermilk

2 tablespoons instant yeast

¼ cup honey

1 egg

1 teaspoon kosher salt

3 to 4 cups all-purpose flour

GOOEY BUTTER CAKE

I can't help but think that in a time of particular stress and sadness, something with the words gooey and butter in the name can only be immensely comforting. This is a made-from-scratch recipe, instead of the cake mix and instant pudding version that has become popular.

:: SERVES 9

FOR THE BASE:

Preheat the oven to 350°F. Line an 8-inch square baking pan with nonstick foil or parchment paper.

Combine the flour and sugar in the bowl of a stand mixer fitted with the paddle attachment. Cut the butter into small pieces and sprinkle over the flour in the bowl. Beat on medium speed until the butter is well mixed with the dry ingredients and resembles rough crumbs. You can use your hands to rub any large clumps of butter into the flour. Sprinkle the mixture over the base of the pan and press in an even, tight layer.

FOR THE FILLING:

Beat the sugar and butter together in the cleaned-out mixer bowl on medium to high speed until light and fluffy. Beat in the egg until well combined. Add the flour in two batches alternately with the evaporated milk until combined. Beat in the corn syrup and vanilla extract until thoroughly combined and smooth. Spread the filling over the base in the pan into an even layer. Bake for 30 to 40 minutes, until the top is golden brown and the center is still a little jiggly. Check the cake about 10 minutes before the time is up to get a feel for when the batter transforms from uncooked to lightly wobbly. Take it out of the oven before the center is firm so you get the gooey.

Remove the pan from the oven and cool completely. Sprinkle the top with confectioners' sugar.

For the Base:

1 cup all-purpose flour

3 tablespoons granulated sugar

6 tablespoons unsalted butter, cold

For the Filling:

1¼ cups granulated sugar

12 tablespoons (1½ sticks) unsalted butter, at room temperature

1 egg

1 cup all-purpose flour

⅔ cup evaporated milk

¼ cup light corn syrup

1 teaspoon vanilla extract

Confectioners' sugar

THE PEARLY GATES

STARTERS AND SNACKS

SWEET TEA PUNCH

The English, when confronted with any type of difficulty or tragedy, instinctively offer a cup of tea, the amount of sugar added being a measure of exactly how dire the problem is. I can't help but think we Southerners do the same thing, only our tea is iced and always sweet. A big jar of Sweet Tea Punch is always a welcome addition to the funeral food table, whether it is served to guests at a visitation or just enjoyed by the family at home.

The best way to make and transport tea is in a gallon pickle jar. For most of my life, I thought gallon pickle jars were some sort of Holy Grail. When ladies brought tea to a party or gathering, they very carefully labeled the jar and asked repeatedly when they could come pick it up. My mother and grandmother would not loan theirs out for fear it would be forever lost. Then I discovered that gallon jars are not the elusive snipe of the glassware world. They are sold everywhere—with pickles in them. I have included a way to use the pickles so you can always have a gallon jar at the ready (see page 40). A jar of these sweet pickles also makes a nice gift.

This is my simplified version of a popular Memphis tea punch. It was traditionally made with two 6-ounce cans of frozen lemonade and limeade, but as far as I can tell, they don't make those anymore. So I use a frozen citrus blend, like pineapple orange.

:: MAKES 1 GALLON

Place the tea bags, mint sprigs, and sugar in a gallon pickle jar or container. Pour 7 cups of boiling water over and stir gently to agitate the sugar. Leave to steep for 10 to 15 minutes, until you have a very dark amber brew. Discard the tea bags and mint. Add the juice concentrate and stir well. Leave to cool slightly, about 20 minutes, then fill the container to the top with cold water. Stir in the extracts and taste for sweetness, adding sugar and orange slices, if desired.

This tea will keep covered on the counter or in the fridge for a few days. Stir well before serving over ice.

4 family-sized tea bags (I prefer the Luzianne brand)

A handful of mint sprigs

¾ cup granulated sugar, plus more to taste

1 (12-ounce) can frozen citrus blend juice concentrate, thawed

1 tablespoon vanilla extract

1 tablespoon almond extract

Water (obviously)

Orange slices, for garnish (optional)

SWEET GARLIC REFRIGERATOR PICKLES

This recipe starts with a gallon jar of pickles, which divides up into many smaller jars (4 quarts, or a combination of smaller sizes). You can also use a quart jar of pickles, which will make three pint jars, and adjust the sugar accordingly.

:: 4 QUART JARS

Pour the pickles into a large colander and drain all the liquid. Rinse out the jar, but do not clean with soap and water. Slice the pickles into ¼-inch pieces. I find doing this by hand the best method, though it takes some time. The pickles are a bit too soft for a mandoline or food processor.

Layer the sliced pickles with the sugar and the garlic cloves and a few good shakes of hot sauce, covering each layer of pickles with sugar before adding more pickles. Fill the jar with sugar as close to the top as you can. Screw on the lid and set aside in a cool place away from direct light. The sugar will dissolve and make a syrup in the jar. Over the next few days, carefully shake the jar to dissolve any sugar that accumulates at the bottom, and add more sugar. Continue to do this for 4 or 5 days, until the syrup covers the pickles and you can't add any more. You may not use the whole 4-pound bag of sugar.

When the pickles are covered in syrup, pour the whole contents of the jar into a large bowl. Discard the garlic cloves. Using a slotted spoon, transfer the pickle slices to very clean Mason jars, pressing down lightly and shaking to distribute the slices evenly. Fill the jars with the pickle slices just to the rim under the screw-on threads. When all your jars are full, evenly divide the syrup into each one. The syrup may not completely cover the pickles, but that's okay. Place the lids on the jars, screw on the bands, and refrigerate. Store in the fridge up to 6 months unopened, or 2 weeks after they have been opened.

1 (1-gallon) jar of whole kosher dill pickles (not pre-sliced)

1 (4-pound) bag of granulated sugar

2 heads of garlic, cloves separated and peeled

Several shakes of good hot sauce

BOURBON BUTTER ROASTED PECANS

There is something quintessentially Southern about a pretty bowl of roasted pecans, be it your grandmother's silver Revere bowl or a funky locally made pottery piece. Roasted pecans are nice to have on the coffee table, by the bar, or on the buffet. And it is easy to make a lovely gift of these nuts by putting them in a decorative tin, a mason jar tied with a ribbon, or a clear plastic gift bag.

Quite by accident, I discovered a brilliant way to produce perfect buttery pecans. I keep my pecans in the freezer, and being in something of a hurry one day, I tossed the frozen nuts into the warm melted butter. The butter and its seasonings clung to the cold nuts, forming a sort of carapace—so there was more butter on the actual nuts than on the baking sheet. Now I use this method for its excellent results.

:: MAKES ABOUT 4 CUPS

Preheat the oven to 300°F. Line a large rimmed baking sheet with nonstick foil.

Melt the butter with the bourbon and hot sauce in a medium bowl in the microwave or in a large saucepan over medium heat. Stir in ½ teaspoon of the salt and the pepper, then quickly stir in the nuts, tossing to coat. Start with a spatula, but as with most things, your good, clean hands are the most efficient tool. Spread the nuts in one even layer on the prepared baking sheet. Roast for 30 minutes, flipping with a spatula every 10 minutes, until the nuts are toasted and fragrant.

Carefully move the nuts on the foil from the baking sheet onto a cooling rack (the heat of the pan will keep toasting them). Cool completely, then store in an airtight container for up to 2 weeks. You can also freeze roasted nuts for up to 3 months.

4 tablespoons (½ stick) unsalted butter

1 tablespoon bourbon

1 teaspoon hot sauce

1 teaspoon kosher salt, divided

¼ teaspoon ground black pepper

1 pound raw pecan halves, frozen for at least an hour

BUTTERMILK BACON STUFFED EGGS

No Southern food spread of any kind—funeral, baby shower, wedding party, holiday celebration, or tailgate—would be complete without a tray of stuffed eggs. My family never calls them deviled eggs because that seems to imply spiciness, and my mother cannot abide spicy. Plus, bringing the devil to a funeral doesn't seem like a very good idea. I make stuffed eggs in all kinds of flavor combinations, but I particularly love this simple version with its quintessential Southern ingredients.

:: MAKES 24 EGGS

12 large eggs

¼ to ½ cup whole buttermilk

5 strips bacon, cooked crisp

2 green onions, light and white green parts

Kosher salt

Generous grinds of black pepper

Place the eggs in a large, deep

The Funeral Fan

In the days before air conditioning was ubiquitous, at any lengthy church service, and funerals were the lengthiest of all, paper fans on wooden sticks were distributed. No one wants Great Aunt Bessie falling out from the heat right in the middle of "The Old Rugged Cross." Shaped like a heart or a shield, the fans were printed with a picture of the deceased and usually a Bible verse of particular relevance, the words to a favorite hymn, even a program for the service. Though the fans have become popular at any event likely to bring out great emotion, they are still generally referred to as "funeral fans."

skillet and cover with water by about an inch. Bring to a boil, and when the water reaches a boil, cook the eggs for 8 minutes. Fill a bowl with ice and water, and as soon as the 8 minutes are up, transfer the eggs to the ice water with a slotted spoon. Leave to cool in the water. Crack the eggshells all over by gently rolling on the counter, then remove the shells. Rinse off the eggs to remove any shell debris and pat dry.

Cut the eggs in half, wiping the knife on a paper towel between eggs so you don't get yolk on the next white. Scoop the yolks into a bowl and place the white halves on a platter or deviled egg plate. Break up the yolks with a fork, and then add the buttermilk a little at a time until you have a smooth and creamy filling. The consistency of your buttermilk will determine how much you need to use. Finely chop 3 strips of bacon and add to the yolks. Mince the green onions finely and add as well. Stir to distribute the ingredients, then salt and pepper to taste. Be generous with the pepper.

Cut the remaining 2 strips of bacon into small pieces and garnish the eggs by pressing a bacon shard into the filling.

EGG AND CAVIAR SPREAD

I decided to include this recipe because it is something I often saw at fancy grown-up parties when I was a child, so it always seemed quite sophisticated to me. When I made this for a party recently to test it for this book, one friend looked at the layer of caviar and said, "This must be for the dead people you really liked." That being said, there is no need to use the finest caviar—the domestic stuff you find at the grocery store is perfectly fine.

:: **SERVES 20**

Place the eggs in a saucepan and cover with water by about an inch. Place over high heat and when the water comes to a boil, cook the eggs for 7 minutes. Fill a bowl with ice and cold water. When the 7 minutes are up, remove the eggs with a slotted spoon to the ice water. Leave to cool for 45 minutes. When the eggs are cooled, roll them on the counter to crack the shells all over and peel. Rinse with cool water to remove any stray shell pieces and pat dry.

Cut the green onions into small pieces and drop in the bowl of a food processor. Add the dill and pulse to break everything up into very fine pieces, scraping down the sides of the bowl a couple of times. Cut the butter into small pieces and add to the bowl, then cut the eggs in half and drop them in the bowl. Add the lemon zest, salt, and pepper and pulse until everything is finely chopped, but with a few larger pieces of egg visible. Add the mayo, a tablespoon at a time, pulsing just until the mixture comes together in a firm paste.

Scoop some of the egg mixture into a 6-inch mold (see note below) and use the back of a slightly dampened spoon to spread it in an even layer. Repeat until all the egg mixture is tightly packed into the mold, then smooth the top and wipe off the edges. Place a piece of plastic wrap directly on the surface of the mixture,

6 large eggs

4 green onions, white and light green parts

¼ cup loosely packed fresh dill fronds

4 tablespoons (½ stick) unsalted butter, softened

1 teaspoon lemon zest

1 teaspoon kosher salt

½ teaspoon ground black pepper

2 to 3 tablespoons mayonnaise

1 (3½-ounce) jar black caviar

then place a small bowl on top to weigh it down. Refrigerate for at least 4 hours, but it will keep for up to 2 days.

Unmold the egg mixture onto a platter and spoon the caviar in an even layer on top. Serve with baguette slices or crackers.

Note: I love to make this in a 6-inch mini springform pan or mini tart pan, but if you don't have one, a small bowl with a flat bottom is fine. Remember you need a flat top to spread the caviar. I've also used a small square glass storage container. Line the bowl with plastic wrap, smoothing it out as much as possible, then fill with the egg mixture and bring the plastic wrap over the top to cover. Unmold and proceed as above.

"[She] epitomized the Southern Lady in her life's three ambitions. As a wife, her support was without limits. As a mother, her love was without condition. As a friend, her hospitality was without distinction."

—Obituary, Columbia, Tennessee

BOURBON PIMENTO CHEESE

I asked a food writer friend of mine what her family considered funeral food, and she responded, "Well, for my big ol' clan of Whiskeypalians, it's got to be something with a little snort in it." So in her honor, I liquored up pimento cheese.

:: MAKES ABOUT 3 CUPS

Drop the green onions and chives in the bowl of a food processor fitted with the metal blade. Pulse a couple of times to chop things up. Add the cream cheese, mustard, Worcestershire sauce, salt, pepper, and paprika and pulse a couple of times. Add the bourbon and blend until smooth, scraping down the side of the bowl once, until you have a smooth paste. Switch to the grating blade and grate the cheeses.

Scrape everything into a large bowl, making sure you scrape out all the bourbon-y paste. Stir the mix a couple of times to combine, then add the pimentos and their juice and the mayonnaise. Stir to completely combine everything, making sure the cheeses are not clumped together and the seasoning paste is well distributed. Cover the bowl and refrigerate for at least 4 hours to allow the flavors to meld. This will keep covered in the fridge for 5 days.

4 green onions, roughly chopped

2 tablespoons roughly chopped chives

4 ounces cream cheese, softened

1 tablespoon prepared yellow mustard

1 tablespoon Worcestershire sauce

½ teaspoon kosher salt

½ teaspoon ground black pepper

½ teaspoon sweet paprika

3 tablespoons bourbon

8 ounces sharp orange Cheddar

8 ounces sharp white Cheddar

8 ounces Havarti

1 (7-ounce) jar diced pimentos

1 cup mayonnaise (preferably Duke's)

LEMON DILL PICKLED SHRIMP

Pickled shrimp is an enduring Southern snack that is eminently useful. Easy to make, it lasts for several days in the fridge. It looks pretty served in a crystal bowl on its own, but can also be served on lettuce as a light meal or salad. And some (I'm not saying who) snack on the shrimp every time the fridge is opened. The traditional recipe can be jazzed up to create a host of flavors—this version is bright with lemon juice, dill, and punchy fennel.

:: SERVES 6 TO 8 ON A BUFFET

Juice 1 lemon, and half of the other if needed, to render ¼ cup lemon juice. Slice the remaining lemon into thin rounds. Whisk the lemon juice, vinegar, and oil together in a large bowl, then whisk in the capers and celery seed. Peel the garlic clove, crush it with a knife, and add to the liquid with the bay leaves, dill, and a couple of sprigs of the feathery fennel fronds.

2 large lemons

1 cup white vinegar

½ cup olive oil

2 tablespoons capers in brine

1 teaspoon celery seed

1 clove garlic

2 bay leaves

4 to 5 sprigs of dill

1 small fennel bulb, thinly sliced

2 pounds raw shrimp, peeled and deveined (21 to 25 count)

Sliced chives, for garnish (optional)

Bring a large pot of water to the boil. Add the shrimp to the water and cook for 4 minutes, then drain and place in a medium bowl that will fit the shrimp snugly. Whisk the pickling liquid a few times and pour immediately over the hot shrimp. The shrimp will not be cooked through, but will continue to "cook" in the acidic marinade. Add the sliced lemons and sliced fennel and stir to coat everything. Press the shrimp down so as much as possible is submerged in the pickling liquid. Place a piece of plastic wrap directly over the shrimp, then put a plate on top to keep the shrimp submerged in the marinade.

Cover the bowl and refrigerate at least overnight, but 3 days is better. Stir a couple of times a day. The shrimp will keep covered in the refrigerator for up to 2 weeks.

To serve, take the bowl from the fridge—the oil may have solidified a bit, but it will loosen up. You can serve directly from the bowl with toothpicks, or lift the shrimp out of the pickling liquid with a slotted spoon. Garnish with chives, if desired.

CRABMEAT MOUSSE, REMOULADE STYLE

Chef Bill Smith, of Crook's Corner in Chapel Hill, North Carolina, commented that any collection of recipes that people make for funerals is bound to be good, because everyone always puts their best foot forward, bringing the dish they are particularly proud of—one that is sure to impress. I think this fits that bill. Elegant and sophisticated, delicate and refined, a molded crabmeat mousse looks impressive on the table.

:: SERVES 20

Pour a little neutral-flavored oil on a paper towel and use it to lightly grease the inside of a 6-cup mold or a bowl. You want the surface slick, but no pooling oil that will show on the unmolded result.

Sprinkle the gelatin in a large mixing bowl and pour over ¼ cup cold water to soften it. Leave for a few minutes, then pour over ½ cup boiling water and whisk until the gelatin is dissolved. Cool to room temperature.

Whisk the mayonnaise, mustard, ketchup, horseradish, lemon juice, chives, and green onions into the gelatin mixture until thoroughly combined. Scrape down the sides of the bowl to make sure all the gelatin is in the liquid. Place in the refrigerator and chill for 20 minutes.

Add the crabmeat to the gelatin mixture and stir well, making sure the crab is broken up and coated with the mixture. Whip the heavy cream to stiff peaks with a mixer. Gently fold the cream into the crabmeat mix, making sure all the ingredients are evenly distributed and combined. Spoon the mousse evenly into the prepared mold, cover with plastic wrap, and refrigerate for at least 5 hours, but up to a day is fine.

When ready to serve, invert the mold onto a platter and leave for a few seconds, then lift the mold off the mousse. Serve with crackers or baguette slices.

1 (¼-ounce) package unflavored gelatin

½ cup mayonnaise

2 tablespoons Creole mustard (such as Zatarain's)

1 tablespoon ketchup

1 tablespoon prepared horseradish, from a jar

1 tablespoon lemon juice

1 tablespoon finely chopped fresh chives

2 green onions, very finely diced

16 ounces lump crabmeat, picked over to remove any stray shells and flaked with a fork

1 cup heavy cream

HOMEMADE MAYONNAISE

It has been something of surprise to me the number of people who, when told I was working on a funeral food cookbook, have said, "Well, of course you'll have a homemade mayonnaise recipe." I wasn't initially planning to, as I think there are plenty of them around. But my mother has insisted—you cannot serve tomato aspic with a dollop of bought mayonnaise—so here is my simple version. Because Mama is always right.

:: MAKES 1¼ CUPS

Place the eggs in a food processor, and add the lemon juice and salt. Process until combined. With the motor running, gradually add the oil in a thin, steady stream. Process until the mixture is creamy, thick, and emulsified. You will actually hear the food processor change sounds from smooth blending to a wet slapping sound. Scrape the mayonnaise into an airtight container. It will keep in the fridge for 3 days.

Note: Use a neutral-flavored vegetable oil like canola or grapeseed. Olive oil adds too distinct a flavor.

2 large egg yolks

1 tablespoon freshly squeezed lemon juice or white wine vinegar

¼ teaspoon salt

1 cup vegetable oil

"Why is it that we rejoice at a birth and grieve at a funeral? It is because we are not the person involved."

—Mark Twain

CUCUMBER RING WITH A SMOKED SALMON CENTERPIECE

I find a certain Sixties chic to this recipe—the lovely ring mold with an enticing centerpiece. But this is all modern and sophisticated without a hint of lime jello or packet seasoning. And it does look pretty and impressive. If you don't have a ring mold, you can use a round-bottomed bowl, and simply surround it with the sliced salmon on the platter.

:: **SERVES 12**

Pour a little neutral-flavored vegetable oil on a paper towel and use it to lightly grease the inside of 6-cup ring mold. You want the surface slick, but no pooling oil that will show on the unmolded result.

Measure ¼ cup of wine into a small saucepan and sprinkle over the gelatin. Cook over medium heat, stirring constantly, until the gelatin is completely dissolved, making sure to scrape down the sides of the pan as needed. Remove from the heat and set aside.

Drop 2 cups of the cucumber (reserving ½ cup) into the carafe of a blender. Add the green onion, buttermilk, mayonnaise, remaining ½ cup wine, lemon juice, dill, salt, and pepper and blend until completely smooth. Pour in the gelatin mixture, making sure to scrape the sides of the pan, and blend for 5 seconds. Stir in the remaining diced cucumber, then pour into the prepared mold. Use a thin spatula to stir and make sure the diced cucumber is evenly distributed in the mold. Cover with plastic wrap and chill for at least 5 hours, but up to 24 is fine.

When ready to serve, invert the mold onto a platter and leave for a few seconds, then lift the mold off the mousse. Cut the smoked salmon into cracker-sized pieces and pile it in the middle of the cucumber ring. Serve with crackers or miniature rye bread slices.

¾ cup white wine, divided

1 (¼-ounce) package unflavored gelatin

2½ cups finely diced cucumber (about 1 seedless English cucumber)

3 green onions, white and light green parts, cut into pieces

½ cup whole buttermilk

¼ cup mayonnaise

¼ cup fresh lemon juice

¼ cup loosely packed fresh dill fronds

¼ teaspoon kosher salt

A few grinds of black pepper

4 to 6 ounces thinly sliced smoked salmon

SWEET POTATO AND PEANUT BUTTER HUMMUS

George Washington Carver was born a slave but became the head of the agriculture department at Alabama's Tuskegee Institute. He was most known for his work on important Southern crops, including peanuts and sweet potatoes. I like to think he'd be pleased with this recipe. On the table with the cakes and casseroles, there needs to be something vegetable-related and healthy. Serve this hummus on a plate of crudités.

:: MAKES ABOUT 1½ CUPS

Preheat the oven to 400°F. Place the sweet potato (or potatoes) on a baking sheet and bake until completely soft, 45 minutes to an hour depending on the size. As soon as the potato is cool enough to handle, pull off the skin; it should be very easy to do this with your fingers. Cool the potato flesh completely.

Place the sweet potato, chickpeas, peanut butter, and garlic in the bowl of a food processor fitted with the metal blade and process a few seconds to break things up. Add the spices, salt, and lemon juice and turn the machine on. Drizzle in the olive oil, and then add the water a tablespoon at a time, until the hummus is smooth and combined.

1 large or 2 small (12 ounces) sweet potatoes

1 (14-ounce) can chickpeas, rinsed and drained

2 tablespoons smooth peanut butter

2 cloves garlic

1 teaspoon cumin

½ teaspoon smoked paprika

Dash of cayenne pepper

1 teaspoon kosher salt

Juice of one lemon (about 3 tablespoons)

3 tablespoons olive oil or green peanut oil

4 to 5 tablespoons water

SMOKY CHEESE WAFERS

I knew there absolutely must be a cheese straw recipe in this book. Because what kind of gathering would it be without little bowls or trays of crispy cheese morsels scattered throughout the room. Most Southerners would still consider these cheese straws, even though they are not put through a cookie press to make the long wavy straws. This method of roll-and-slice is just so much easier. I changed things up a bit by using smoked cheddar cheese and smoked paprika, which makes these just a little bit mysterious, but will still satisfy the cheese straw need. Look for naturally smoked cheddar instead of smoked flavor added or smoked processed cheese. I find it regularly at better grocery stores. The recipe works with regular cheddar but obviously won't have that hint of smoke.

:: **MAKES ABOUT 3 DOZEN**

8 ounces naturally smoked Cheddar

16 tablespoons (2 sticks) unsalted butter, cold

2 cups all-purpose flour

1 teaspoon kosher salt

½ teaspoon smoked paprika

½ teaspoon Worcestershire sauce

2 to 3 tablespoons buttermilk or heavy cream

Grate the cheese and the cold butter together in a food processor. Switch from the grating blade to the metal blade, then add the flour, salt, paprika, and Worcestershire sauce. Process until the dough just begins to come together and looks moist and grainy. With the motor running, drizzle in the buttermilk until the dough begins to pull away from the sides and form a ball.

Cut two lengths of waxed paper, divide the dough into two portions, and place each one on a waxed paper length. Form these into two logs and roll them tightly, pressing in to form nice solid logs. Twist the ends like a candy wrapper. Refrigerate the logs for at least an hour before baking, but you can refrigerate them for 2 days or freeze them for 3 months.

When ready to bake, preheat the oven to 350°F and line two baking sheets with parchment paper. Remove the rolls from the fridge and slice into medium-thick wafers, about ¼ inch each. Flatten with the tines of a fork, if desired, for decoration.

Place them on the baking sheet with a little room to spread, and bake until golden around the edges and firm on the top, about 10 to 12 minutes. Cool on the pans for a few minutes, then remove to wire racks to cool.

"Hi Everyone. I'm at my Final Destination. It took me 89 years, 5 months, and 6 days, but I finally made it. God walked me to the mansion and I didn't lose my breath one time! . . . I invite you all to my celebration of life. . . . Be sure to come, especially if it's a workday. This will be one celebration you don't want to miss."

—*Obituary, Nashville, Tennessee*

SALTINE TOFFEE

This is an oldie but a goodie—a stalwart community cookbook recipe and a classic food gift. And there is a reason for that. It is sweet and salty and crunchy and easy to make, and incredibly comforting. I'm not reinventing the wheel here, just bumping up the classic with a little vanilla and a sprinkle of salt. But I wanted to share this because I get requests for a batch of it from friends all the time, and it was a special treat much appreciated in the last months of a friend's mother's life.

:: MAKES ABOUT 100 PIECES

Preheat the oven to 400°F. Line a 12-by-18-inch rimmed baking sheet with nonstick foil or parchment paper. Lay the crackers out in one layer as close together as possible, filling the baking sheet.

Melt the butter, brown sugar, and vanilla in a medium saucepan over medium heat, stirring frequently. When the butter is melted, raise the heat and bring the mixture to a boil, and keep at a boil for 3 minutes, stirring occasionally. When the 3 minutes are up, give it a good stir and pour evenly over the crackers on the baking sheet. Spread the caramel around with a spatula if needed, but don't worry if the surface isn't covered completely—you just don't want it pooling in one place. Bake the crackers for 5 minutes, then remove from the oven and immediately sprinkle the chocolate chips over the top in an even layer. Let sit for 5 minutes, then use a flexible, preferably offset, spatula to spread the chocolate in an even layer over the crackers. If you'd like to, sprinkle the pecans and/or the sea salt evenly over the top of the toffee. Leave to cool, then place in the refrigerator for about an hour for the chocolate to set. Break into pieces and store in an airtight container for 5 days.

About 50 saltine crackers

16 tablespoons (2 sticks) unsalted butter

1 cup dark brown sugar

1 teaspoon vanilla extract

12 ounces semi-sweet chocolate pieces

1 cup finely chopped pecans (optional)

Flaky sea salt, such as Maldon (optional)

THE ETERNAL GARDEN

FRUIT AND VEGETABLES

CORN BREAD SALAD

Black-eyed peas and corn bread are an essential food group of Southern cuisine, and it would be remiss of me to leave them out of this book. This quintessential Southern layered salad is colorful and hearty, plus it looks beautiful on the table, can be made ahead, and serves a crowd.

:: SERVES 15 TO 20

FOR THE CORN BREAD:

Preheat the oven to 425°F. Grease an 8-inch square baking pan.

Whisk the cornmeal, flour, sugar, baking powder, salt, and pepper together in a medium mixing bowl. Stir in the egg, buttermilk, and oil until the batter is well combined, with no dry ingredients visible. Spread the batter into the prepared pan and bake for 25 minutes, until firm and lightly golden and a tester inserted in the center comes out clean. Cool completely.

The corn bread can be made up to 1 day ahead and kept covered loosely with a tea towel on the counter. Day-old corn bread soaks up the dressing nicely.

FOR THE BUTTERMILK DRESSING:

Whisk all the ingredients together in a medium bowl. Cover and refrigerate for at least 2 hours, but this can be made a day ahead.

FOR THE SALAD:

Place the frozen corn in a colander and run warm water over it to thaw, then leave to drain completely.

Put the black-eyed peas in a pot covered with water and bring to a boil. Cook until just tender, about 15 to 20 minutes. Whisk together the oil, vinegar, mustard, and salt and pepper, to taste. Drain and rinse the peas, then put back into the pan and pour over the vinaigrette. Leave to cool.

For the Corn Bread:

1 cup coarse yellow cornmeal

1 cup all-purpose flour

¼ cup granulated sugar

4 teaspoons baking powder

1 teaspoon kosher salt

½ teaspoon ground black pepper

1 egg

1 cup whole buttermilk

¼ cup vegetable oil

For the Buttermilk Dressing:

1 cup whole buttermilk

1 cup mayonnaise

1 large clove of garlic, put through a press or very finely chopped

1 teaspoon lemon juice

1 teaspoon salt

½ teaspoon ground black pepper

½ teaspoon celery salt

½ teaspoon dried dill

¼ teaspoon ground mustard

1 tablespoon chopped fresh parsley

1 tablespoon chopped fresh chives

For the Salad:

2 (12-ounce) bags frozen corn

2 (14½-ounce) bags frozen black-eyed peas

3 tablespoons olive oil

3 tablespoons cider vinegar

1 teaspoon Dijon mustard

Salt and ground black pepper, to taste

2 bell peppers (a mix of colors is pretty), finely chopped

1 pint cherry tomatoes, halved

6 strips bacon, cooked and crumbled

2 cups grated Cheddar

Cut the corn bread into small chunks. Cover the bottom of a 4-quart glass bowl with the corn bread, then spoon over the black-eyed peas in an even layer. Next layer on the corn, then the bell peppers, then the tomato halves, cut side down. Sprinkle over the bacon, then spread the cheese in an even layer. Top the salad with the buttermilk dressing, spreading it out to cover the top completely and seal the salad.

Cover the bowl and refrigerate for at least 4 hours, but up to 24. Toss the salad before serving.

"He had a life-long love affair with deviled eggs, Lane cakes, boiled peanuts, Vienna [Vi-e-na] sausages on saltines, his homemade canned fig preserves, pork chops, turnip greens, and buttermilk served in martini glasses garnished with corn bread."

—Obituary, Gulfport, Mississippi

SOUTHERN THREE BEAN SALAD WITH BACON VINAIGRETTE

Church supper, dinner on the ground, funeral reception—there you will find the ubiquitous three bean salad, most often made with canned green beans, canned kidney beans, canned wax beans, and bottled dressing. I veer a little more to the Southern here, with field peas and lima beans, and pull it all together with a bacon vinaigrette. But the spirit of the dish is the same, only it's fresher and crisper. My dad was a fan of three bean salad, and I like to think he'd approve of this version.

:: SERVES 8 TO 10

FOR THE SALAD:

Fill a Dutch oven half full with water and add the frozen field peas. Bring to a boil, then reduce the heat to medium-low and simmer for 10 minutes. Add the lima beans and cook a further 10 minutes. Taste each to see that they are cooked but not completely soft. For a cold pea salad, you want a little bite, so don't let them get mushy. Drain the peas and limas and place them in a large bowl. Fill the pot with water again, bring to a boil and add the green beans, and cook for 5 to 7 minutes, until just cooked and tender but still with a little bite. Drain the beans and cool, then cut into small pieces. Add the green beans to the peas in the bowl and chill in the fridge for 30 minutes.

Cut the bacon into small pieces and cook until crispy, then remove to paper towels to drain. Save ¼ cup of the drippings for the dressing and set it aside to cool, but not solidify. You can use the rinsed out pot you used for the beans.

For the Salad:

12 ounces frozen purple hull peas

12 ounces frozen baby lima beans

12 ounces frozen French-style green beans

6 slices bacon, cooked until crispy

1 (7-ounce) jar diced pimentos, rinsed and drained

4 green onions, white and light green parts, finely chopped

1 pound bacon

¼ cup bacon drippings, not solidified

½ cup vegetable oil

4 tablespoons cider vinegar

1 tablespoon sorghum or dark honey

1 teaspoon hot sauce (or more to taste)

Generous grinding of black pepper

Add the drained pimentos and chopped green onions into the bowl with the chilled peas and toss to combine. Pour over the dressing.

FOR THE VINAIGRETTE:

In a jar with a tight-fitting lid, mix all the ingredients and shake vigorously to emulsify the dressing, making sure the sorghum is blended in. Pour the dressing over the peas and stir to coat. You may not want all the dressing at first, but save any remainder as you may want to add some right before serving. Taste the salad and add some salt if needed. These peas tend to need quite a bit.

Chill the salad until ready to serve. Toss the crumbled bacon into the salad right before serving. The salad (without the bacon) will keep for up to 2 days covered in the fridge.

PIMENTO CHEESE MACARONI SALAD

I never really thought of macaroni salad as a funeral food until I was attending a wedding at a very, very small church in a very, very small Mississippi town. As I was waiting in the vestibule to be ushered down the aisle, I glanced at the church bulletin board and saw a sign-up sheet for the funeral reception of a congregation member. Three people had signed up to bring macaroni salad.

:: **SERVES 10**

Cut the bacon into small pieces and cook over medium-high heat until very crispy. Remove to paper towels to drain and reserve 2 tablespoons of the bacon grease.

10 strips bacon

1 pound elbow macaroni

4 tablespoons cider vinegar, divided

7 green onions, white and light green parts only

3 tablespoons chopped chives

3 tablespoons chopped parsley

1½ cups whole buttermilk

1 cup sour cream

1 tablespoon Worcestershire sauce

1½ teaspoons kosher salt

1 teaspoon ground black pepper

12 ounces sharp Cheddar, grated

2 (7-ounce) jars diced pimentos, rinsed and drained

Mary

Mary and her husband had to go to a work event at the home of someone they did not know. It was after dark and the lighting in the old neighborhood was not very good as they were looking for the street address. So they went to the house with the cars parked outside and people streaming in. They walked in and introduced themselves, but couldn't help but notice the mood was rather somber. Finally, the woman who appeared to be the hostess approached them, and as they tried to make small talk, it became clear that this was in fact her daughter's wake. Mary and her husband politely said I'm sorry for your loss and slowly backed out of the party. Mary's first response as she walked through the door, "Thank goodness we hadn't eaten any of the food yet!"

Cook the macaroni in a large pot of water with 2 tablespoons vinegar according to the package instructions until cooked through. Drain the pasta, rinse it with cool water, and drain well again. Return the pasta to the pot and add the remaining 2 tablespoons of cider vinegar and the 2 tablespoons of bacon grease. Stir to coat the pasta well and leave to sit for 15 minutes.

Place 4 of the green onions, the chives, and the parsley in a food processor or blender (I like the mini-food processor for this) and pulse to chop finely. Add the buttermilk, sour cream, Worcestershire sauce, and salt and pepper, and blend until smooth and combined. Pour the dressing over the macaroni and stir gently to coat. Add the grated cheese, drained pimentos, and cooked bacon and stir to distribute. Finely chop the remaining green onions and add to the salad, stirring to combine. The dressing will absorb and thicken as it chills, so don't worry if it looks a little loose. Taste for seasoning and adjust as needed. Cover the salad and refrigerate until chilled. The salad will keep for 3 days covered and refrigerated. You can stir in a little more buttermilk to loosen the salad up before serving.

FIRE AND ICE TOMATOES

Fire and Ice Tomatoes is a recipe that has always been in my consciousness. How it got in my mind, I can't imagine, because as I child I would never have eaten anything even resembling a raw tomato. The original recipe, to the best of my knowledge, is from The James K. Polk Cookbook, *produced by the James K. Polk Memorial Auxiliary of Columbia, Tennessee, in 1978. Columbia is the town my mother grew up in, and President Polk had a home there that is now a historical site. My aunt served on the committee that produced the wonderful* Provisions and Politics, *a follow-up to the original Polk cookbook, published in 2003. The book is a collection of new and fresh recipes, with a few old favorites thrown in. When she started with the project, my first question was, "It will include Fire and Ice Tomatoes, right?" Neither my mother nor my aunt had any idea what I was talking about—they had to be reminded of the recipe. So how it became a part of my recipe memory bank, I will never know. But I do know that it is good. And it's the perfect take-along recipe—it can happily sit in its container in the fridge to be served up and snacked on for days, yet retains its fresh, crisp profile.*

The original recipe says these tomatoes will keep in the fridge up to 3 days, but I happily keep them up to 5.

:: SERVES 6 TO 8

Cut the tomatoes into quarters and place in a 9-by-13-inch glass or ceramic dish. Finely dice the onion and sprinkle over the tomatoes. Core, seed, and remove the ribs of the bell pepper and cut into thin strips (if the pepper is long, cut the strips in half). Scatter the pepper strips over the tomatoes and onions.

6 large ripe, red tomatoes

1 yellow onion

1 green bell pepper

¾ cup white wine vinegar

¼ cup cold water

1½ teaspoons mustard seed

1½ teaspoons granulated sugar

1½ teaspoons celery salt

½ teaspoon salt

⅛ teaspoon cayenne pepper

⅛ teaspoon ground black pepper

In a saucepan, combine the vinegar, water, mustard seed, sugar, celery salt, salt, and peppers. Bring to a boil, stirring, and boil for 1 minute. Immediately pour the hot vinegar mixture over the tomatoes, then stir gently to combine. Leave the tomatoes to cool slightly, then cover with plastic wrap and refrigerate. Leave to marinate for several hours, stirring occasionally.

Serve on its own as a salad or a side dish or atop some lettuce leaves.

TOMATO ASPIC

I don't think I have ever seen a table at a Southern visitation without Tomato Aspic. Tomato aspic is made in a mold, and these molds can vary from person to person. My mother has a whole collection of aspic molds, from plain round to fancy. Party aspic is generally formed in a ring mold so the center can be mounded up with shrimp, chicken salad, mayonnaise (homemade, of course), artichoke hearts—you name it, someone has put it in the center of an aspic. This party tomato aspic is always served on a silver tray, usually resting on a bed of lettuce leaves, with parsley around the edge of the tray. It also provides the rare chance to use the silver aspic server that was a wedding gift, or inherited from a grandmother; a silver handle with a flat, round or slightly pointed surface, sometimes plain, sometimes intricately etched.

I will be honest here, I am not a huge fan of tomato aspic. I am a polite Southern girl, though, and always eat it when it is put in front of me. However, I do feel that for full Southern lady credentials, you have to be able to make an aspic. The recipe below is the version I prefer, tailored to my own tastes, with a nice celery tang and plenty of tomato flavor and a minimum of the truly odd ingredients you sometimes see in old recipes. Members of my family are dedicated aspic eaters and they have always given this a thumbs-up.

:: SERVES 12

Lightly brush a 5-cup ring mold with flavorless vegetable oil. This is a vital step—baking spray doesn't work well.

Place 2 cups of the tomato juice in a small bowl and stir in the gelatin to dissolve. Set aside. Pour the remaining tomato juice into a large saucepan, add the remaining ingredients (except for the parsley), and stir to combine. Bring to a boil, reduce the heat, cover the pan and simmer for 10 minutes.

Strain the juice into a bowl with a pouring spout. Press on the solids to release any juice, then discard. Whisk in the reserved gelatin mixture until thoroughly combined. Carefully pour into the prepared ring mold, filling as full as possible.

Very carefully transfer the mold to the refrigerator. When the aspic has cooled, cover the mold with plastic wrap, then chill until firm, at least 8 hours or overnight.

Unmold the aspic onto an elegant tray, and surround with parsley.

5¾ cups (46 ounces) tomato juice

3 (¼-ounce) packets unflavored gelatin

½ medium onion, chopped

½ cup chopped celery leaves

2 tablespoons Worcestershire sauce

1 tablespoon granulated sugar

1 teaspoon celery salt

1 teaspoon salt

Parsley, for garnish

Meredith

Meredith's mother died in the small town she and her family grew up in, and her children had long ago moved away. Meredith and her sisters returned for the funeral and the days of visits from family and friends, but returned to their own homes and jobs shortly after. A few weeks later, the sisters all gathered at her mother's house to clean everything out. Meredith opened the refrigerator to find it empty, save for one shining, glistening, molded, congealed salad, green and made with cream cheese and whipped topping—left just where it had been put when someone brought it. As Meredith told me, "That thing could have survived a nuclear war."

THE JELLO MOLD

The idea of a molded jello salad can strike fear into the hearts of men. We scoff now, but for so many years, gelatin mold salads were an absolute mainstay, in fact the pride and joy, of any hostess's table. So they can't be all bad. It is simply not possible that millions of women served up dishes for decades that absolutely no one liked. When my grandmother died, one of the lovely ladies who had cared for her in her last years brought us a rather shockingly purple gelatin salad covered in creamy topping. We were all extremely dubious about the dish, which also included whole grapes, but my mother and my aunt insisted we each try at least one bite since the lady had been nice enough to make it and deliver it to the house. So we each scooped the smallest possible spoonful onto our plates and tentatively tasted it—and it was delicious. We all went back for seconds and scraped the dish clean.

Molded salads with meat date back to medieval times, but the advent of packaged gelatin powder in the 1890s made it possible for any cook to quickly create a spectacular presentation, or to stretch leftovers by folding them into a molded salad. Flavored, pre-sweetened gelatin is where I think things went off the rails a little. Asparagus molded in lime jello? Olives and chicken in orange-flavored gel? I leave that behind for fresh flavors molded with simple, plain gelatin. Writing this book has given me a new-found appreciation for the humble congealed salad. With the right ingredients, they make a very pretty presentation anyone should appreciate.

SUNSHINE SALAD

Everyone could use a little sunshine in a dark time. This congealed version is a little old-school twist on the ever-popular carrot and raisin salad. I promise, it's good.

:: **SERVES 6 TO 8**

Drain the pineapple through a sieve set over a small bowl or measuring cup. Press on the pineapple pulp to extract all the juice. Set the pineapple aside. Juice the orange and the lemon and add to the pineapple juice. You should have 1 cup of juice, but if not, make up the difference with cold water.

Whisk the gelatin and sugar together into a medium mixing bowl and slowly pour over the boiling water. Stir to fully dissolve the gelatin, then stir in the 1 cup of juice until combined. Place the bowl in the refrigerator for 45 minutes to an hour until it begins to set.

Grate the carrots on the fine holes of a box grater. Finely grated carrot mixes better in the salad and is more pleasant to eat. Don't use pre-grated, purchased carrots, which are too thick and tough. When the gelatin mixture has cooled and begun to set, stir in the reserved pineapple, the carrots, pecans, and raisins. A fork will help distribute the crushed pineapple and carrot shreds more evenly. Spread the mixture into an 8-inch square glass dish, using the fork to make sure the ingredients are distributed, cover with plastic wrap, and chill until set, at least 2 hours.

Sunshine Salad can be made up to 3 days ahead and kept covered in the fridge.

To serve, cut squares of the salad and, if desired, dollop with a little whipped cream or mayonnaise.

1 (8-ounce) can crushed pineapple

1 large navel orange

1 large lemon

2 (¼-ounce) packets unflavored gelatin

¼ cup granulated sugar

1 cup boiling water

3 carrots, peeled

½ cup chopped pecans

½ cup raisins

Whipped cream or mayonnaise, for garnish

CRANBERRY SALAD

A truly classic congealed salad, this is a verved up version of the one my aunt made for Thanksgiving for many years, chock-full of cranberries, celery, apple, and Southern black walnuts—and no red dye number three jello. I like to add pomegranate juice to get that deep red color, but cranberry juice works as well.

:: **SERVES 12**

Whisk the gelatin and sugar together in a medium mixing bowl. Bring the pomegranate juice to a boil in a small saucepan, then pour it over the gelatin mixture. Stir until the gelatin and sugar are dissolved. Stir in the cold apple cider until combined. Refrigerate the bowl for 35 to 40 minutes, until the mixture is beginning to set.

Place the cranberries in the bowl of a food processor. Cut the celery and apple into chunks and drop in the bowl. Grate the orange zest into the bowl, then cut away the peel and white pith. Cut the orange flesh into pieces and add to the bowl, then pulse to finely chop everything, scraping down the sides of the bowl a couple of times.

Scrape the chopped fruits into the gelatin in the bowl and stir to thoroughly combine. Stir in the chopped walnuts, then pour the mix into a 13-by-9-inch dish. Cover with plastic wrap and refrigerate for several hours until firm.

3 (¼-ounce) packets unflavored gelatin

½ cup granulated sugar

1½ cups pomegranate or pure cranberry juice

2 cups apple cider, chilled

12 ounces fresh cranberries

3 stalks celery

1 medium green apple, cored

1 medium navel orange

½ cup walnut pieces, preferably black walnuts

COLLARD AND SPINACH MADELEINE

There is something comforting about a creamy baked spinach dish. Spinach Madeleine is a classic Southern version, which, I think, first appears in River Road Recipes *from the Junior League of Baton Rouge. It adds a little spicy kick, traditionally with jalapeño roll cheese, which is no longer manufactured. My version has an extra layer of Southern flavor with the addition of collard greens into the mix, and replaces the processed cheese with spicy pepper jack.*

:: SERVES 8 TO 10

2 (14-ounce) packages frozen chopped collards

2 (10-ounce) packages frozen chopped spinach

8 tablespoons (1 stick) unsalted butter

8 green onions, white and light green parts, finely chopped

2 garlic cloves, finely minced

¼ cup all-purpose flour

1 cup heavy cream

1 cup cooking liquid

12 ounces pepper Jack, cut into small cubes

2 teaspoons kosher salt

2 teaspoons Worcestershire sauce

1 teaspoon ground black pepper

1 teaspoon hot sauce

½ cup plain dry breadcrumbs

Put the collards and spinach in a large pot and cover with water. Bring to a boil, reduce the heat, and simmer for 15 minutes. Drain the greens in a large colander, reserving 1 cup of the cooking liquid. Press out as much liquid as you can from the greens with a spatula or back of a spoon.

Wipe out the pan and then melt the butter over medium heat. Add the chopped green onions and cook until they are soft and wilted, about 3 minutes. Add the garlic and cook for 1 more minute. Sprinkle over the flour and stir until everything is combined and you have a thick paste. Slowly add the cooking liquid while stirring constantly, then continue stirring while adding the cream. Stir until the sauce is thick and smooth and bubbling. Stir in the cheese cubes, a little at a time, until melted and smooth. Stir in the salt, Worcestershire sauce, pepper, and hot sauce. Stir in the collards and spinach, making sure to separate the greens, and that they are fully coated with the sauce. You can use a fork to separate the leaves, if needed.

Spoon the greens into to a 3-quart baking dish. Sprinkle the breadcrumbs in an even layer over the casserole. At this point, the dish can be cooled, covered, and refrigerated. When ready to bake, preheat the oven to 350°F. Bake the casserole until heated through and bubbling, about 30 minutes.

"[The mother of four children] . . . died peacefully while in the loving care of her two favorite children. All her breath leaked out of her."

—*Obituary, Raleigh, North Carolina*

GREEN BEAN CASSEROLE WITH TARRAGON AND HAZELNUTS

When I initially put my mind to the idea of funeral foods, the first dish that came up was the ominously nicknamed dish "funeral beans." Mention that to any Southerner and they will know exactly what you are talking about. Canned green beans, canned soup and fried bits of something. Green Bean Casserole picked up the name "funeral beans" because it is often taken to the bereaved. Though why it is thought kind to inflict that on the distressed, I cannot fathom.

I cannot abide the standard version. It is a sulfurous, chemical abomination to me. But use fresh green beans and bright, herbal tarragon and you've really got something. Crunchy hazelnuts add a nice touch, and a hit of cream, tangy mayonnaise and nutty cheese keep things in the traditional vein, while the lemon keeps it from being too cloying.

:: SERVES 8

Preheat the oven to 350°F. Butter an 8-inch square baking dish.

Cut the trimmed green beans into roughly 1-inch pieces. Bring a large skillet of water to a boil and drop in the beans. Boil for about a minute, just until the bright color of the beans comes out. Drain the beans and plunge into a bowl of ice water to cool. Drain again.

Wipe out the skillet and melt the butter over medium-high heat. Add the shallot strands and cook, stirring frequently, until the shallot is soft and just beginning to turn a pale caramel brown, about 4 minutes. Add the hazelnuts, stir, and cook for about 2 minutes, then stir in the garlic and cook for a further minute. Do not let the garlic brown. Remove the pan from the

2 pounds fresh green beans, trimmed

4 tablespoons (½ stick) unsalted butter

4 shallots, halved and sliced into thin half moons

½ cup chopped hazelnuts

2 cloves garlic, finely minced

3 teaspoons chopped fresh tarragon

Zest and juice of one lemon

Salt and ground black pepper, to taste

¼ cup mayonnaise

¼ cup heavy cream

6 ounces Gruyère, grated

heat and stir in the green beans, tarragon, the lemon zest, 2 tablespoons lemon juice, and salt and pepper to taste, until everything is evenly distributed. Set aside to cool.

Mix the mayonnaise and cream together in a small bowl, then add this to the green beans, stirring to coat well. Spread a layer of beans in the baking dish, sprinkle over half the cheese, and layer the remaining beans and cheese.

Cover the dish with foil and bake for 20 minutes. Remove the foil and bake a further 10 minutes. Serve immediately.

The casserole can be prepared several hours before baking and kept covered in the refrigerator.

FUNERAL BAKED BEANS

After a lifetime of eating baked beans at barbecue restaurants, I searched high and low for a version to make myself. A close friend, finally, after much prodding, wrote out her "secret" recipe on a sheet of monogrammed notepaper, which I still have in my files. Her version used canned pork and beans, but I eventually changed it up to use a mix of plain canned beans and a tangier homemade sauce. When I told her I was writing a book about funeral food, she immediately said, "You know, those baked beans are a funeral recipe." That's how she thinks of this recipe, because it first came to her from her mother, who'd eaten the beans at a funeral and left with the recipe, which she was told was a funeral staple for that family. My friend's mother then started making them for funerals and passed the recipe on to her daughter and to many others.

This recipe makes a HUGE batch of beans, perfect for a hungry crowd. The recipe is easily halved, or extras freeze well. You can make the beans a day before serving them and keep them in the fridge. Reheat the dish over low heat in the pot, or better yet, scoop the beans into a casserole dish and reheat them in the oven. I love the subtlety of cane syrup, but molasses, sorghum, or maple syrup works as well. And, of course, they are excellent with Slow Cooker Pulled Pork with Homemade Barbecue Sauce (page 124).

:: SERVES 15

1 pound bacon

3 cups chopped onions (about 2 large onions)

1 cup ketchup

¾ cup apple cider vinegar

½ cup dark brown sugar

¼ cup cane syrup, sorghum, or molasses

2 teaspoons dry mustard powder

1 teaspoon salt

1 teaspoon ground black pepper

2½ cups apple cider or pure apple juice

8 (16-ounce) cans of beans—a combinations of kidney beans, red beans, pinto beans, great northern beans, or navy beans (black beans do not work), rinsed and drained

The Home-Going and the Celebration of Life

Life in the rural South, particularly for people of color, was often hard and grinding. So in the particular way Southerners have of combining sorrow and joy, funeral services, or the gatherings after them, are seen as a celebration of the deceased moving to a better place free from trouble, or going home to heaven to be with Jesus. The services often include prayers, a eulogy and scripture readings, even a sermon reminding the mourners that it is time to get right with God. But these events also involve joyous song, jokes about the deceased, and a general sense of celebration.

Cut the bacon into small pieces, place in a large Dutch oven, and sauté over medium-high heat until crispy. Remove the bacon from the pan with a slotted spoon to drain on paper towels. Drain off half of the bacon drippings (reserve for another use). Leave the bacon grease to cool a little bit, then put the onions in the pot and sauté until soft and translucent. If you drop the onions into the blistering hot grease, they will fry and be crispy, not soft and caramelized.

Meanwhile, whisk together the ketchup, vinegar, sugar, syrup, mustard powder, salt, and pepper in a small bowl. When the onions are soft, pour in the sauce and stir to coat. Cook until bubbling and the sugar is melted. Pour in the apple cider and stir until heated through.

Drop the drained beans into the pot and stir carefully to coat with the sauce. Stir in half the crisped bacon. Bring the pot to bubbling, then lower the heat, cover and simmer for 1 hour, stirring occasionally to prevent the beans from sticking. Stir carefully or the beans will break up and become mushy. Near the end of the cooking time, stir in the remainder of the bacon.

THAT PINEAPPLE THING

The first step in undertaking a cookbook such as this is asking every single person you encounter what they think of when they think "funeral food." To my surprise, several of my deeply rooted Southern friends answered "that pineapple thing." Somehow, I knew immediately what they were talking about, for this is truly a Southern standard. You'll find this recipe in almost every Southern community cookbook, sometimes in the dessert section, sometimes in the side dish section, often alongside ham recipes. Cheesy Pineapple Casserole, Scalloped Pineapple, sometimes just Pineapple Casserole, it is there in the dog-eared, worn pages of favorite cookbooks. I'll be honest here, before this project I had never made this, or even thought of making it, but with a preponderance of evidence that this qualifies as a truly Southern casserole, I had to give it a try. And like everyone else, I was surprised to find that I really do like it.

:: **SERVES 6 TO 8**

1 (20-ounce) can crushed pineapple

1 (20-ounce) can pineapple chunks

1 cup granulated sugar

6 tablespoons self-rising flour

½ teaspoon kosher salt

8 ounces sharp Cheddar, grated

40 buttery crackers, such as Ritz (that's about 1 sleeve)

8 tablespoons (1 stick) unsalted butter, melted

Drain the crushed pineapple and the chunks over a bowl to catch the juice. Whisk the sugar, flour, and salt together in a medium mixing bowl, then add the grated cheese. Toss the cheese around to separate any clumps, making sure all the cheese is coated with the sugar mixture. Add both pineapples and stir to combine, making sure there are no dry ingredients visible in the bowl and that everything is well mixed. Spread the pineapple in an even layer in a well-greased 2-quart baking dish.

Put the crackers into a zip-top plastic bag and crush with your hands until you have fine crumbs, with a few larger pieces lingering. Rinse and dry out the bowl, then mix the crumbs with the melted butter and ¼ cup of the reserved pineapple juice. Spread the crumb topping evenly over the top of the casserole.

At this point, the casserole can be covered and refrigerated for up to a day. When ready to serve, preheat the oven to 350°F. Bake for 25 to 30 minutes until hot through and bubbly and golden on the top. Serve warm.

"He loved Southern food smothered in cane syrup . . . he hated vegetables and hypocrites. [He] adored the ladies. . . . A few of the more colorful ones were Momma Margie, Crazy Pam, Big Tittie Wanda, Spacy Stacy, and Sweet Melissa [he explained that nickname had nothing to do with her attitude]. He attracted more women than a shoe sale at Macy's. He got married when he was 18, but it didn't last. [He] was no quitter, however, so he gave it a shot two more times."

—*Obituary, Bloomingdale, Georgia*

AMBROSIA WITH ROSEMARY AND HONEY SYRUP

Ambrosia was the fruit that the gods of Mount Olympus ate to ensure immortality, so taking it to a funeral might be shutting the barn door when the horse is already out. But the beautifully layered citrus is a piece of Southern culinary history that should be enjoyed more often. Many Southerners associated ambrosia with Christmas, because that's when the citrus fruits became readily available. I stick with the truly classic version, not the creamy Cool Whip and marshmallow calamity that followed. The most traditional ambrosia recipes call for oranges, coconut, and a little sugar, but I think a combination of pink-hued grapefruit and bright-tinged oranges looks very pretty indeed, and if I find blood oranges in the market, I use those too, even tangerines or satsumas. Freshly grated coconut is a wonderful addition, but I now find unsweetened flaked coconut readily available and sometimes use the big curls found at health food stores, which is just so much easier. Pineapple makes a nice addition, and I buy the precut pieces from the produce section. To make things interesting and a bit more modern, I sweeten the lot with a honey syrup tinged with rosemary. A glass bowl of ambrosia is a lovely feature for any buffet table.

:: SERVES 10

¼ cup honey

¼ cup granulated sugar

¼ cup water

3 sprigs fresh rosemary

3 red grapefruit

4 oranges

8 ounces fresh pineapple

1 cup unsweetened flaked coconut

Sit the honey, sugar, and water together in a small saucepan and heat over medium-high heat. Bring to a boil and cook for about 8 minutes, until the sugar is dissolved and the syrup has thickened. Drop in the rosemary sprigs and push down to submerge in the syrup, then cover and cool completely. The syrup can be made up to a day ahead.

Cut the tops and bottoms from the grapefruit, and place the now flat end on a cutting board. Use a sharp knife to cut away the peel and all white pith from the fruit, then use the knife to divide the fruit into sections. Do the same with the oranges. Cut the pineapple into bite-sized chunks. In a large glass bowl, make a layer of mixed grapefruit, orange, and pineapple, then sprinkle over half the coconut and drizzle over half the syrup. Top with another layer of fruit and the remaining coconut, and drizzle the last of the syrup over all. Cover with plastic wrap and refrigerate for up to 4 hours.

"She is survived by her loving husband and sons, her sister . . . her brother . . . her bossy daughter-in-law and three as yet unspoiled granddaughters . . . and numerous relatives who were all loved but not mentioned in the will."

—*Obituary, Hot Springs, Arkansas*

PARTY POTATOES

I have made these countless times for Christmas Eve and New Year's Eve parties, making three or four batches to feed the crowds. The frozen diced potatoes are the trick, saving the work of peeling and cubing pounds of potatoes. This creamy, cheesy version is the essence of comfort food and the perfect gift for a bereaved family.

:: SERVES 12

Grease a 9-by-13-inch baking dish. Shake the potatoes into a colander and leave to thaw for about 15 minutes. There is no need to thaw them completely, but make sure there are no ice crystals.

Cut the bacon into small pieces and cook until crispy. Remove to paper towels to drain and cool.

Break up the potatoes and toss with the bacon pieces, cheese, and chives in the baking dish, doing your best to evenly distribute everything.

Melt 4 tablespoons butter in a medium saucepan, then whisk in the flour. Cook until smooth and pale in color, then slowly stir in the milk. Stir constantly until the sauce has thickened, then stir in the salt, pepper, garlic powder, onion powder, paprika, and cayenne. Cook, stirring, until the mixture thickens and comes to a boil. Pour over the potatoes in the baking dish, spreading it out to cover the surface. Melt the remaining 2 tablespoons butter and cool slightly. Crush the crackers in a zip-top plastic bag, add the butter and shake to combine—get in there with your hands to mix everything up if needed. Spread the crumbs over the top of the casserole.

At this point, the dish can be cooled, covered, and refrigerated overnight. When ready to bake, preheat the oven to 350°F. Uncover the dish and bake for 50 to 60 minutes, until the mixture is set and the top is lightly golden.

1 (2-pound) package frozen Southern-style hash-brown potatoes (small, cubed potatoes, no onions or seasonings)

8 strips bacon

8 ounces sharp Cheddar, grated

¼ cup finely chopped chives

4 tablespoons (½ stick) unsalted butter, plus 2 tablespoons

3 tablespoons all-purpose flour

3 cups whole milk

1½ teaspoons kosher salt

Ground black pepper, to taste

½ teaspoon garlic powder

½ teaspoon onion powder

½ teaspoon paprika

Dash of cayenne

About 30 buttery crackers (like Town House), 1 sleeve

BUTTERMILK MACARONI AND CHEESE

There are nine million was to make macaroni and cheese, but this one will stand out because of the creamy tanginess provided by the buttermilk. It is also easy to make because you don't have to cook a sauce first.

:: SERVES 6 TO 8

Bring a Dutch oven full of well-salted water to a rolling boil and add the macaroni. Give it a good stir, then cook 1 minute less than the package instructions, about 10 minutes. Drain and rinse with cold water.

While the noodles are cooking, whisk the eggs in a large bowl that will hold the pasta and the cheese, then whisk in the buttermilk, mustard, salt, pepper, and spices and whisk until smooth and thick. Reserve 1 cup of the grated cheese for the top of the dish, then stir the remaining cheese into the buttermilk mixture. Stir in the noodles until well coated with sauce.

Grease a 13-by-9-inch baking dish with baking spray, and spread the macaroni and cheese in the prepared dish. Sprinkle the reserved cheese over the top. The mac and cheese can be prepared to this point up to a day ahead, cooled, covered, and refrigerated.

When ready to bake, preheat the oven to 350°F. Take the dish from the fridge and let it come close to room temperature. Bake until heated through and bubbly, about 30 minutes.

16 ounces elbow macaroni

3 eggs

2 cups whole buttermilk

1 tablespoon Dijon mustard

1½ teaspoons salt

1 teaspoon ground black pepper

1 teaspoon onion powder

1 teaspoon garlic powder

1 teaspoon sweet paprika

1 pound sharp Cheddar, grated

24 HOUR SALAD

24 Hour Salad is a mainstay for the Southern church supper table. Fresh and relatively healthy, it makes a beautiful presentation layered up in a pretty glass trifle bowl. And best of all, it can be made ahead. Cover the top with a creamy dressing and just toss right before serving.

:: SERVES 12

FOR THE SALAD:

In a 4-quart glass bowl, layer the ingredients in the order listed. Start by scattering them around the edge of the bowl, so the pretty layers are visible, then fill in the center. Remember when preparing the ingredients that you'll want bite-sized pieces that are easy to spear with a fork.

FOR THE DRESSING:

Place the green onions, garlic, chives, dill, and parsley in a food processor or blender (I like to use the mini–food processor for this) and pulse to chop finely. Add the mayonnaise and salt and pepper, and blend until smooth and combined. Dollop the dressing evenly over the surface of the salad and use a spatula or the back of a spoon to spread the dressing to completely cover the top of the salad, making sure to go all the way to the edges of the bowl, sealing all the ingredients under the dressing.

Cover the salad with plastic wrap and refrigerate for at least 4 hours, but up to 24. Toss the salad immediately before serving.

For the Salad:

5 cups of green leaf lettuce, torn into bite-sized pieces

3 cups of baby spinach

6 hardboiled eggs, chopped

3 bell peppers (a mix of colors is pretty), chopped

1 large English cucumber, chopped

3 tomatoes, chopped

8 ounces sharp Cheddar, grated

1 (12-ounce) bag frozen peas, thawed and drained

For the Dressing:

2 green onions, white and light green parts, roughly chopped

1 garlic clove

¼ cup roughly chopped chives

½ cup roughly chopped dill

2 tablespoons parsley leaves

2 cups mayonnaise

½ teaspoon kosher salt

½ teaspoon ground black pepper

TOMATO PUDDING

The term "pudding" in Southern cooking does not just apply to desserts—corn pudding, carrot pudding, and this tomato pudding being the prime examples. I like the old-fashioned, homey name for this, though it is sometimes called scalloped tomatoes. And this dish is a perfect example of a few simple ingredients coming together to make a surprisingly complex and delicious whole.

:: SERVES 6

Spray a 2-quart baking dish with baking spray.

Cut the bread into thick slices and toast in the oven at 350°F just until crispy, about 5 minutes. Don't let the bread get brown or burned, just firm and crispy. Cut the toasted bread into bite-sized pieces.

Open the can of tomatoes, and using scissors, cut down into the can to snip the tomatoes into small pieces. Heat the olive oil in a skillet over medium heat and add the onion. Cook until the onion is soft and glassy, then add the butter and let it melt. Stir in the flour until it is well combined, then pour in the tomatoes and their juice. If there are any large pieces left, just snip them with the scissors. Add the brown sugar and stir to combine. Reduce the heat and simmer for 10 minutes, stirring occasionally. Stir in the basil, salt, and pepper, then fold in the bread cubes until coated with sauce. Spoon the tomato pudding into the prepared dish.

At this point, the dish can be cooled, covered, and refrigerated for up to a day.

When ready to cook, preheat the oven to 350°F, Cook the tomato pudding until warmed through and bubbly, about 45 minutes.

4 ounces soft Italian bread

1 (28-ounce) can whole peeled tomatoes

2 tablespoons olive oil

1 cup finely diced onion (about 1 medium onion)

2 tablespoons unsalted butter

2 tablespoons all-purpose flour

¼ cup light brown sugar

1 tablespoon chopped fresh basil

1 teaspoon salt

Generous grinds of black pepper

THE GOSPEL BIRD

CHICKEN

FRIED CHICKEN

Across the board, people of all ages, races, religions, genders, and regions of the South have answered my question, "What do you think of as funeral food?" with "Fried Chicken." So below I offer my blueprint for perfect Southern fried chicken—according to me. If your family has a cherished recipe, by all means use it.

My Rules:

❖ First, you must marinate the chicken in buttermilk so the meat is moist and tender.

❖ You have to season the chicken well. I use an old method of making a chicken shake—my own seasoning blend that I mix up in batches and sprinkle on the chicken before flouring.

❖ The grease needs to start hot and stay hot. And it should be shortening, maybe with some bacon grease thrown in.

❖ The chicken needs to be left alone with the grease to come to an understanding.

:: MAKES 8 PIECES OF CHICKEN

Measure all the spices into a small bowl and whisk to combine. Store in an airtight jar, preferably one with a shaker top.

Place the chicken parts in a large zip-top plastic bag (or two). Pour over the buttermilk to cover the chicken completely. Throw in some good hot sauce and lightly shake the bag around to cover all the chicken pieces and distribute the hot sauce. Place the bag on a tray or plate to catch any spills and refrigerate overnight.

A couple of hours before you are ready to fry, take the chicken out of the fridge and place the pieces on a rack over a sheet pan. Sprinkle both sides of the chicken liberally with the chicken shake. Be very generous. Let the chicken sit so it begins to come closer to room temperature. Shortly before frying, scoop a generous amount of flour into a paper sack or a plastic bag. Place each

For the Chicken Shake:

4 tablespoons sweet paprika

4 tablespoons kosher salt

4 teaspoons garlic powder

2 teaspoons ground black pepper

1 teaspoon onion powder

1 teaspoon smoked paprika

½ teaspoon cayenne pepper

For the Chicken:

1 whole cut-up fryer chicken, 8 pieces of chicken

2 to 3 cups buttermilk

Several shakes of hot sauce

Flour

chicken piece in the sack and shake it around to coat it with flour. Get in there with your hands to sprinkle and press flour into all the crevices and parts of the chicken. Pick up each piece and shake off any loose flour and place back on the rack.

Scoop the shortening into a large, high-sided cast-iron skillet set over medium-high heat. Allow the shortening to melt and the hot grease to heat to 325°F. Increase the heat under the skillet slightly, then add the chicken pieces. Put the thighs in the middle of the pan and the breasts and the legs around the outside. Fry the chicken until golden brown on the first side, about 12 minutes before you even think about turning it over. Check a few times to make sure the oil is still around 325°F and adjust the heat accordingly. Flip the chicken—it should be easy to do with no resistance or sticking. If it's not, leave it another minute or so. Cook on the second side for another 12 minutes without moving. The chicken should be crispy and brown and cooked through—that's a 170°F internal temperature. Remove the cooked chicken to a clean rack set over a pan to drain. Do not use the same one you had the raw chicken on unless it has been thoroughly cleaned.

Serve hot, at room temperature or cold.

Note: This recipe for chicken shake makes much more than is needed for one batch of chicken but it will store in an airtight container. It is also a great seasoning for hamburgers or for any chicken—grilled or oven-fried—that you make.

Feel free to cut up the chicken yourself, though I always get the folks at the store to do it for me. You can fry as many batches of chicken as you want, just clean out any bits from the grease, add more shortening and bring the grease back up to temperature.

OLD FASHIONED CHICKEN SALAD WITH COOKED DRESSING

Over the years, as I peruse my ever-growing collection of community cookbooks, I've run across a number of recipes for "Cooked Dressing for Chicken Salad." Rarely is there an actual recipe for chicken salad, just for the dressing. After seeing so many recipes, though, I had to give the salad a try. And I am glad I did. The dressing is creamy and tangy with a sweet-and-sour edge from the sugar and vinegar. I kept the recipe simple here, with crunchy celery and almonds and a nice herbal note from parsley, but this salad will absolutely work with a variety of additions, so get creative. I assure you, it will be the most unique chicken salad on the table.

:: SERVES 6

3 chicken breasts

1 cup chicken broth

1 lemon

3 celery stalks

1 bay leaf

2 eggs

²/₃ cup granulated sugar

2 tablespoons all-purpose flour

½ cup water

½ cup white wine vinegar

½ teaspoon salt

2 tablespoons unsalted butter

½ cup slivered almonds

3 tablespoons finely chopped parsley

Salt and ground black pepper, to taste

Place the chicken breasts in a large saucepan that fits the breasts in one layer and pour over the broth. Squeeze the lemon juice into the pot, then drop in the juiced skin. Break up 1 celery stalk and add it to the pan with the bay leaf. Add enough water to cover the chicken breasts if needed, then place over high heat and bring the liquid to a boil. Reduce the heat to low, cover the pan, and simmer until the chicken is cooked through (a 165°F internal temperature), about 10 to 12 minutes. Remove the chicken breasts to a plate to cool.

Make the dressing while the chicken is cooling. Beat the eggs in a medium saucepan, then beat in the sugar. Stir the flour into the water in a small bowl to make a paste, then add it to the eggs. Add the vinegar and salt and stir to fully combine. Cook over medium heat, stirring constantly, until the dressing thickens to the consistency of runny pudding. Pull the pot off the heat, and stir in the butter a small piece at a time, letting each one melt before adding the next. Set aside to cool slightly.

Finely chop the remaining 2 stalks of celery and place in a large bowl. Dice the chicken into small pieces and add them and the almonds and parsley to the bowl, and stir to combine. Spoon in the dressing a bit at a time and stir to coat the chicken until you have a consistency that suits you. You may not want to use all the dressing.

Season with salt and pepper to taste, cover and chill until ready to serve. The salad will keep for 2 days.

CLASSIC CHICKEN SALAD WITH GRAPES AND POPPY SEEDS

Chicken salad is a wonderful thing to take to a friend in need. It can be transferred to a lovely bowl and served with crackers to any unexpected guest, it's perfect to make sandwiches for visiting family, and frankly is a nice thing to have around for snacking on straight out of the fridge when there is just no will to cook. This is my version of the classic Southern tearoom chicken salad, with a rich dressing and a perfect combination of savory and sweet, crunchy and creamy.

:: SERVES 6

3 boneless skinless chicken breasts

1 cup white wine

1 cup chicken broth

1 sizable bunch fresh tarragon, divided

6 ounces red seedless grapes

3 green onions

½ cup chopped pecans

1 teaspoon poppy seeds

½ teaspoon kosher salt

Ground black pepper, to taste

½ cup heavy whipping cream

1 cup mayonnaise

Place the chicken breasts in a pan and pour over the wine and broth. Add enough water to cover the chicken. Measure out ¼ cup loosely packed tarragon leaves and set aside, then drop the rest into the pan. Bring to a boil, then lower to a simmer, cover the pot, and cook until the chicken is cooked through, reaching an internal temperature of 165°F, about 20 minutes. Remove to a plate to cool.

Cut the grapes into quarters and place in a large mixing bowl. Finely mince the green onions and add to the bowl. Mince the remaining ¼ cup tarragon leaves and add to the bowl, then add the pecans, poppy seeds, salt, and pepper. Chop the chicken into small bite-sized pieces and drop in the bowl, then toss well to combine everything.

Beat the heavy cream in a medium mixing bowl with a mixer into very stiff peaks. Add the mayonnaise and fold it in gently, until the cream and mayo are thoroughly combined. Pour the dressing over the chicken in the mixing bowl and stir to coat everything well and to distribute the ingredients evenly. Refrigerate immediately, and leave for a few hours to let the flavors meld. The salad will keep covered in the refrigerator for 3 days.

HOT CHICKEN SALAD

Sometimes, during periods of grief or stress, what is needed is comfort. No need for bold, unique flavors or technical preparations, just good, solid comfort food. Enter the hot chicken salad. The stalwart of ladies, luncheons, and church potlucks, this is the classic casserole no one can resist. I can resist, however, the canned condensed soup called for in most recipes. Instead I make a simple cream sauce to thicken up the mix. Now, you could go more elegant with the topping, using buttered breadcrumbs or leaving it off altogether, but the classic crushed potato chips do create a salty crunch that makes this dish special.

:: SERVES 6 TO 8

Preheat the oven to 350°F. Place the chicken breasts in a baking dish, cover with foil, and bake until the chicken is cooked through, 20 to 30 minutes. The internal temperature should register 165°F on a meat thermometer. When the chicken is cool enough to handle, dice it into small pieces and place them in a large bowl.

Meanwhile, melt the butter in a small saucepan, then whisk in the flour until a smooth paste forms. Cook, stirring constantly, for a few minutes to cook out the floury taste. Pour in the chicken broth and stir until it bubbles and any lumps of flour have disappeared. Remove from the heat and stir in the heavy cream until smooth. Season with salt and pepper and set aside to come to room temperature.

Toast the almonds in a large dry skillet over medium-high heat until lightly browned and nutty-smelling. Add to the chicken in the bowl. (You can skip the toasting and add the nuts plain, but this step does add a lovely layer of flavor). Add the diced celery and shallots to the bowl and toss everything to combine. Add the cream sauce, sour cream, mayonnaise, and lemon juice and stir

4 boneless, skinless chicken breasts

2 tablespoons unsalted butter

3 tablespoons all-purpose flour

¾ cup chicken broth

¼ cup heavy cream

Salt and ground black pepper, to taste

1 cup slivered almonds

2 cups finely diced celery (about 5 or 6 stalks)

½ cup finely diced shallot (about 2 shallots)

1 cup sour cream

1 cup mayonnaise

2 tablespoons fresh lemon juice, from one lemon

1 pound sharp white Cheddar, grated, divided

1 cup crushed plain potato chips (I like Ruffles)

until everything is combined and well mixed. Stir in 1 cup of the grated cheese, a teaspoon of salt, and generous grinds of black pepper and stir to combine.

Spread the mixture in a well-greased 9-by-13-inch baking dish then sprinkle the remaining cup of cheese evenly over the top. Spread the crushed potato chips evenly over the cheese. The casserole can be made up to this point, covered, and refrigerated for up to 2 days. When ready to serve, preheat the oven to 350°F. Remove the casserole from the fridge while the oven is heating, then bake until hot through and bubbly, about 30 minutes.

"It pains me to admit it, but apparently, I have passed away. Everyone told me it would happen one day but that's simply not something I wanted to hear, much less experience. Once again I didn't get things my way! That's been the story of my life all my life."

—*Obituary, Phillips, Florida*

HOMEMADE SALSA VERDE CHICKEN AND RICE

A few years back, the hot dish on the shared meal circuit was a salsa verde chicken casserole made with jarred salsa, rotisserie chicken, and instant rice. It appeared at book clubs, supper clubs, family dinners, and on the doorsteps of those in need of a delivered meal. I've had it many times and always enjoyed it, though I'm not much of a fan of jarred salsa or rotisserie chicken. But I recently started whipping up a little quick salsa verde for myself to keep in the fridge as a dip for veggies and baked tortilla chips as a quick and healthy snack. It occurred to me that maybe I would be more interested in that casserole if I made it with the fresh salsa verde and freshly cooked chicken. So I put together this version, and it has been a hit.

This recipe for salsa verde makes about 2 cups, which is more than is needed in cooking the dish. I like to serve the extra for diners to spoon on top of their portions, but it also makes a great dip that could be served beforehand with tortilla chips. This recipe is not particularly spicy, but if that's the way you like things, add a seeded, diced jalapeno or two when sautéing the chicken.

:: SERVES 6

FOR THE SALSA VERDE:

Preheat the broiler in the oven. Husk the tomatillos, rinse them and dry with paper towels. Line a rimmed baking sheet with foil (nonstick is best) and spread the tomatillos on the sheet. Broil for 5 minutes until brown and blistered. Use tongs to turn the tomatillos and blister on the other side, about 5 more minutes.

Place the onion, cilantro, and garlic in the bowl of a food processor. When the tomatillos are blistered, use the tongs to lift them into the bowl, leaving any accumulated liquid behind. Pour over the lime juice and process until you have a textured puree, with no large chunks left. Taste and add salt as needed. Cool completely, transfer to an airtight container and refrigerate for up to 4 days.

For the Salsa Verde:

1 pound tomatillos (about 10)

½ yellow onion

¼ cup packed cilantro leaves

2 cloves garlic

¼ cup freshly squeezed lime juice

Salt, to taste

3 cups chicken broth

1 cup salsa verde

2 cups long grain white rice

½ teaspoon salt

3 chicken breasts

1 tablespoon olive oil

1 (4-ounce) can diced green chiles

3 green onions, chopped

1 clove garlic, minced

2 cups milk

5 tablespoons all-purpose flour

8 ounces Monterey Jack, grated, divided

1 cup (8 ounces) sour cream

FOR THE CASSEROLE:

Stir the broth and salsa verde together in a medium saucepan, add the rice and salt and stir to combine. Bring the broth to a boil and let it boil for about 15 minutes, until the liquid is evaporated and little steam vents form on the surface. Remove from the heat, cover the pot, and leave to sit for 5 to 10 minutes.

While the rice is cooking, cut the chicken into small, bite-sized pieces. (I like to do this with scissors.) They will shrink some when cooking, but you want to distribute the chicken evenly throughout the casserole, so no big chunks. Put the olive oil in the bottom of a Dutch oven, then add the chicken. Drain some of the liquid off of the green chiles and add them to the pot with the chopped green onions. Cook over medium-high heat, stirring frequently, until the chicken is cooked through, about 10 minutes. Add the minced garlic and cook a further 2 minutes.

Pour ½ cup of milk into a 4-cup measuring jug, then add the flour and whisk until you have a smooth paste. Add the remaining milk (to the 2¼ cup line) and whisk until smooth and incorporated. Pour the milk into the pot with the chicken and stir. Cook, stirring frequently, until the sauce has thickened, about 10 minutes, then remove the pan from the heat and add in most of the cheese (hold back about ½ cup to put on the top of the casserole) and the sour cream, and stir until everything is well combined and the cheese is melted.

Fluff the rice with a fork, making sure the salsa verde is evenly distributed, then add the rice to the pot with the chicken and sauce, and stir so that all the rice is coated and everything is evenly distributed. Taste and add salt if needed.

Scrape the chicken and rice into a well-greased 9-by-13-inch casserole dish and smooth the top. Spread the remaining cheese over the top of the casserole. At this point, you can cool, cover, and refrigerate the dish for up to a day.

When ready to serve, preheat the oven to 350°F and bake the casserole until warmed through and bubbling, about 40 minutes. Serve with the remaining salsa verde to top.

PAPER BAG CHICKEN WITH HOMEMADE GREEK SEASONING

I have friends who refer to this as "funeral chicken" and friends who call it "new baby chicken," so I think it covers the full spectrum of life. It's a perfect dish to take to anyone who needs a meal, simple to make but packed with flavor and eminently useful. It's never a bad thing to have some leftover roasted chicken in the fridge. The usual recipe for this chicken uses a certain popular Greek seasoning that is sold in a yellow shaker, but I like to start fresh to avoid MSG and other additives. This recipe makes a bit more seasoning than you need, but it will keep in an airtight jar for more chickens or to sprinkle on other meats or roasted potatoes and vegetables. I ask for an extra unused paper bag from the store (don't use the one you bring the groceries home in, in case there has been a spill or leak). I've never had an issue with the bag burning or singeing, just make sure it doesn't touch the surfaces of the oven.

:: SERVES 6

FOR THE SPICE MIX:

Measure everything into an airtight jar and shake well to combine. If you have a spice grinder, feel free to give this a whirl to make it a little more finely textured.

FOR THE CHICKEN:

Position a rack in the lower third of the oven. Preheat the oven to 400°F. Place a standard brown paper grocery bag on its side on a rimmed baking sheet.

Pat the chicken dry with paper towels, then rub the butter all over the outside of the chicken in an even, thick layer. Stuff any extra butter in the cavity of the chicken. Sprinkle the spice mix

For the Spice Mix:

2 teaspoons kosher salt

2 teaspoons dried basil

2 teaspoons dried oregano

2 teaspoons garlic powder

1 teaspoon ground black pepper

1 teaspoon dried dill

1 teaspoon dried marjoram

1 teaspoon dried parsley flakes

1 teaspoon ground rosemary

½ teaspoon ground cinnamon

½ teaspoon ground thyme

½ teaspoon ground nutmeg

For the Chicken:

1 (3-to-4 pound) roasting chicken

4 tablespoons (½ stick) unsalted butter, softened

in a thick, even layer over the entire chicken. Place the chicken in the bag on the baking sheet and fold the top closed as tightly as possible. Place the baking sheet in the oven, making sure nothing touches the sides or the heating element. Cook the chicken for 1½ hours, then check that the internal temperature has reached 165°F. Remove the chicken to a platter or foil pan. Wrap it in foil to keep it warm for delivery, or let it cool and refrigerate it, loosely covered.

CELERY SEED CHICKEN

Poppy seed chicken is a classic comfort food casserole, creamy and simple with appeal for everyone. I make poppy seed chicken with leftover cooked chicken all the time. But I once found myself with chicken but no poppy seed, so I made a quick substitution with celery seed and found I liked this accidental version better than the original. I never thought the poppy seed added much anyway, but the celery seed definitely does—just a little hint of mystery. And I love the tang that buttermilk adds.

:: **SERVES 6**

Preheat the oven to 350°F. Place the chicken in a baking dish and cover with foil, Bake for 20 to 30 minutes, until it reaches an internal temperature of 165°F. When cool enough to handle, dice the chicken into small pieces.

Melt the butter over medium heat in a deep skillet large enough to hold the chicken. Whisk in the flour until smooth. Add the milk, whisking constantly, then the buttermilk, and bring to a low bubble. Cook, whisking, until thickened. The sauce may appear a little curdled, but that's just fine. Stir in the chicken, the sour cream, and the vinegar until combined, then stir in the celery seed. Taste and add salt and pepper as needed.

Scrape the chicken into a greased, 2-quart baking dish and smooth the top. Spread the cracker crumbs in an even layer over the casserole. At this point, the dish can be cooled, covered, and refrigerated for up to a day before baking.

When ready to cook, preheat the oven to 350°F. Bake until hot through and bubbling around the edges, about 30 minutes.

3 boneless, skinless chicken breasts

4 tablespoons (½ stick) unsalted butter

¼ cup all-purpose flour

1½ cups whole milk

¾ cup buttermilk

¼ cup sour cream

1 teaspoon white wine vinegar

1 tablespoon celery seed

Salt and ground black pepper, to taste

1 cup crushed buttery crackers (about 20 crackers; I like Ritz)

HOMEMADE CHICKEN SPAGHETTI

When the idea for a book on funeral food was first proposed to me, I knew casseroles would play a major role. And this is the first casserole that came to mind. In its most recognizable form, "Ro-Tel Spaghetti" is perhaps the most popular take-along casserole in the Southern canon. Though traditionally made with the namesake canned combination of tomatoes and peppers and several cans of creamed soup, I've left that behind for a fresh, rich, totally from-scratch version that is completely recognizable but with deeper flavor and creaminess. You'll probably have a little more chicken meat than you need; consider it a bonus.

:: **SERVES 6**

Place the chicken breasts, carrot, celery stick, onion, 4 cloves of garlic, and bay leaves in a large Dutch oven and cover with 12 cups of water. Bring to a boil, then reduce the heat to medium-low, cover, and simmer for an hour.

While the chicken is cooking, roast the poblano peppers. You can either place the peppers on the grate of a gas stove directly over the flame, turning frequently until charred and blackened all over, or you can place the peppers on a roasting rack a few inches from the broiler in the oven, turning frequently, until black all over. When the peppers are charred, either place them in a paper bag and roll the top closed or in a small bowl covered with plastic wrap. When the peppers are cool enough to handle, peel off the skin and rinse under cool water to remove all traces of the skin. Split the peppers open and remove the seeds and cut out any membrane. Finely chop the pepper flesh and set aside.

Remove the chicken from the pot and set aside. Remove the vegetables, garlic, and bay leaves with a slotted spoon and discard. Reserve 3 cups of the cooking liquid for the sauce. Bring the rest of the liquid in the pot back to a boil and add the spaghetti, giving

4 bone-in, skin-on chicken breasts

1 carrot

1 celery stick

½ onion

6 garlic cloves, divided, 2 minced for the sauce

2 bay leaves

2 poblano peppers

3 cups reserved chicken cooking liquid

8 ounces spaghetti, broken in half

4 tablespoons (½ stick) unsalted butter

7 green onions, finely chopped

½ teaspoon cumin

3 tablespoons all-purpose flour

1 (8-ounce) block of cream cheese, cubed and at room temperature

3 plum tomatoes, seeded and chopped

2 cups Cheddar, finely grated, divided

Salt and ground black pepper, to taste

it a good stir. Cook a minute less than the package recommends, about 10 minutes, then drain the pasta and rinse with cold water.

Rinse and dry the pasta pot and return it to the stove. Melt the butter over medium-high heat, then add the green onions and cook until soft and translucent, about 5 minutes. Add the 2 minced garlic cloves and the cumin and cook 1 minute more. Sprinkle over the flour and stir until the onions are coated and thick. Whisk in the reserved cooking liquid and cook, stirring, until thickened, about 10 minutes. Whisk in the cream cheese, a bit at a time, whisking well after each addition. It may look a bit separated or curdled at the beginning, just keep whisking and it will smooth out. When all the cream cheese is smooth, stir in 1 cup of the grated cheese and whisk until smooth. Season well with salt and pepper.

Pull the meat from the chicken breasts, discarding any skin or membrane, and shred with two forks. Stir the pasta and 3 cups of chicken into the sauce in the pan, stirring to coat completely and distribute everything evenly. Gently fold in the chopped tomatoes and poblanos. Taste and add more salt if needed. Spread the mixture into a well-buttered 9-by-13-inch baking dish, smoothing the top to an even layer. Sprinkle the remaining 1 cup of cheddar cheese over the top. At this point, the casserole can be cooled, covered, and refrigerated overnight.

When ready to cook, preheat the oven to 350°F and bake the casserole, covered with foil, for 30 minutes or until it is hot through and bubbling. Remove the foil and bake a further 5 minutes to completely melt the cheese on top. Serve immediately.

JAMBALAYA CASSEROLE

This Louisiana inspired chicken and rice casserole adds a little jazz to the standard casserole list. I love having the flavors of jambalaya in a make-ahead, buffet-friendly version.

:: SERVES 8

FOR THE CREOLE SEASONING:

Place all the ingredients in a small jar and shake well to combine.

FOR THE CASSEROLE:

Cut the chicken breasts into small bite-sized pieces (I like to use scissors), place them on a plate and sprinkle with 1 tablespoon of the creole seasoning. Leave chicken to sit while you get on with things.

Cut the bacon into small pieces (again, scissors are handy) and place in a Dutch oven over medium-high heat. Cook until the bacon is crispy, then remove it to a plate or bowl lined with paper towels to drain. While the bacon is cooking, finely dice the onion, bell pepper, and celery. Cut the sausage in half lengthwise, then into pieces about as thick as a nickel.

When you remove the bacon from the pot, drop in the chicken pieces and cook for a few minutes until just sealed and lightly browned. Remove the chicken back to the plate with a slotted spoon. Drop the sausage into the pan and cook until it is browning, getting crispy, and beginning to curl up. Remove with a slotted spoon to paper towels. Drain away all but ¼ cup of the fat. Add the diced onion, pepper, and celery to the remaining fat, sprinkle over another tablespoon of creole seasoning, then sauté over medium heat until the onion is soft and translucent, about 10 minutes. Add the tomato paste, tomatoes, and bay leaves and continue cooking for another 2 minutes. Pour in the wine and broth and stir, scraping any browned bits from the bottom of the pan. Bring the sauce to simmer, then return the chicken to the

For the Creole Seasoning:

1 tablespoon kosher salt

1 tablespoon sweet paprika

1 tablespoon garlic powder

1 tablespoon ground black pepper

1½ teaspoons ground thyme

1 teaspoon onion powder

¾ teaspoon ground oregano

For the Casserole:

3 boneless, skinless chicken breasts

12 ounces bacon

1 medium yellow onion

1 green bell pepper

1 celery stalk

1 pound andouille sausage

1 tablespoon tomato paste

1 (14½-ounce) can petite cut diced tomatoes

2 bay leaves

1½ cups white wine

3 cups chicken broth

1 cup long grain white rice

2 (15-ounce) cans red beans, rinsed and drained

½ cup dry breadcrumbs

pot. Stir in the sausage and rice to combine well and bring back to a low bubble. Cover the pot and cook for 15 minutes, stirring, until the rice is tender and some of the liquid has been absorbed. Bring back to a simmer and drop in the beans and the cooked bacon and stir. Remove the bay leaves and simmer for 10 minutes. Leave to cool. At this point, the mixture will be a little soupy, but the liquid will be absorbed as it rests. Spoon the casserole into a 9-by-13-inch pan. Sprinkle the breadcrumbs evenly over the casserole.

The casserole will keep wrapped tightly up to 2 days in the fridge.

When ready to cook, preheat the oven to 350°F. Place the dish on a baking sheet and cook for 15 minutes until heated through.

HOT BROWN CASSEROLE

The classic hot brown sandwich is a particular favorite of mine—how could anyone resist a turkey sandwich blanketed in a creamy, cheesy sauce and crispy bacon. I've transformed the sandwich into a feeds-a-crowd, make-ahead casserole, perfect for a gathering.

:: SERVES 8

Cut the bread into rough bite-sized cubes and spread out on a baking sheet or tray. Leave to dry for a few hours (but not until crisp or hard). Spray a 13-by-9-inch baking dish thoroughly with baking spray.

Cut the bacon into small pieces and cook until crispy. Remove with a slotted spoon to a paper towel–lined plate to drain.

Cut the turkey into small pieces, then shuffle them through your fingers to separate them. Measure out 1 cup of mixed grated cheese and set aside for the topping. Layer half the bread cubes in the baking dish, then spread over half the turkey, half the remaining cheese, and half the bacon. Top with another layer of bread cubes and the remaining turkey.

Mix the eggs, milk, Dijon mustard, hot sauce, salt, and pepper together in a large bowl and whisk thoroughly, or blend until smooth in a blender. Pour the milk mixture over the bread cubes slowly, making sure it is evenly covering the bread cubes. Push the bread cubes down into the mixture to cover. Let the casserole sit for at least 30 minutes to soak up much of the liquid while you make the topping. Press down on the bread with a spatula occasionally so it can soak up the milk.

12 ounces soft-crust Italian bread

1 pound bacon

1½ pounds deli turkey, sliced about ¼-inch thick

8 ounces Swiss cheese, grated

8 ounces Cheddar, grated

10 eggs

4 cups whole milk

3 tablespoons Dijon mustard

1 teaspoon hot sauce

1 teaspoon kosher salt

Generous grinds of black pepper

For the Topping:

2 tablespoons unsalted butter

2 tablespoons all-purpose flour

2 cups whole milk

½ teaspoon salt

¼ teaspoon nutmeg

1 cup grated cheese, reserved from the casserole

Bacon remaining from the casserole

FOR THE TOPPING:

Melt the butter in a saucepan, then whisk in the flour. Cook until you have a smooth, pale paste, then slowly whisk in the milk. Cook, stirring frequently, until the sauce has thickened and is smooth. Whisk in the salt and the nutmeg. Stir in the cheese until completely melted. Set aside to cool to room temperature.

When the sauce has cooled, and the bread has soaked up a great deal of the liquid, spread the sauce in an even layer over the casserole, all the way to the edges of the dish. Sprinkle over the last of the cheese and the bacon and lightly press into the sauce. Cover with foil and refrigerate for at least 8 hours, but overnight is fine.

When ready to cook, preheat the oven to 400°F. Take the dish out of the fridge to take the chill off while the oven is heating. Place the dish on a baking sheet in case of overflow. Cook casserole, covered, for 40 minutes, then remove the cover and cook for an additional 10 minutes, until it is set and puffed up and the topping is bubbly and golden.

"When the preacher came to Sunday dinner, as he did in some houses with astonishing frequency, and the gospel bird was served, he always laid claim to the preacher's parts [the best parts of the chicken]. He inevitably left the bony parts to the family of the house."

—Jessica Harris, *The Welcome Table*

CROWNING GLORY

MEAT

BAKED HAM WITH SWEET TEA GLAZE

I always look for a bone-in, fully cooked, not sliced, smoked city ham with no water added. Sliced hams tend to dry out when being reheated and water-added hams can have a spongy texture. And a ham bone is a great thing to have around for cooking greens or making soup. Sometimes I order online from wonderful Southern smokehouses or go to a local meat market.

:: SERVES A CROWD

Preheat the oven to 325°F. Place the ham on the rack of a roasting pan (I use the one that came with my oven). Use a sharp knife to score a diamond pattern in the top of the ham, about 1 inch deep and ¼ inch apart. Pour 2 cups of water into the bottom of the roasting pan, then bake the ham for 2½ to 3 hours, about 20

For the Ham:

1 (7- to 8-pound) bone-in half ham, unsliced

For the Glaze:

1½ cups water

3 garlic cloves

2 black tea bags

4 sprigs fresh mint

¾ cup light brown sugar

2 tablespoons cider vinegar

City Ham

We distinguish in the South. City ham is your standard Easter ham, wet-cured or brined, then smoked and sold fully cooked, it just needs to be warmed through, though a glaze is certainly worth it.

Country Ham

The most glorious of the Southern meats, country hams are dry-cured with salt and sugar, hung and aged for months or years. Some are smoked as well. A whole country ham needs to be soaked and boiled before serving, though many smokehouses sell ready-to-eat center-cut slices or small pieces cut biscuit-sized.

minutes per pound, until the internal temperature of the thickest part of the ham reaches 130°F. I like to insert a probe thermometer with an alarm, so I can get on about my business until the alarm sounds.

Brush the top and sides of the ham with half the glaze and bake for a further 20 minutes, then finish with the remaining glaze and another 10 minutes in the oven.

Remove the ham to a large cutting board and cover loosely with foil. The ham can be sliced and served warm, or left to cool then refrigerated, covered, for up to 3 days.

FOR THE GLAZE:

Bring the water to a boil in a medium saucepan with a lid. Peel the garlic cloves and crush with the flat side of a knife. Remove the pan from the heat and add the tea bags, garlic cloves, and mint. Cover the pan and leave to steep for 30 minutes.

Fish out the tea bags, garlic, and mint, then add the brown sugar and vinegar and return to a medium-high heat. Cook the glaze, stirring frequently, until it has reduced by a little more than half and is thick and syrupy, about 20 minutes. Keep the glaze warm over low heat.

SLOW COOKER HAM WITH BROWN SUGAR AND BOURBON

If the big, bone-in city ham is too much, here's a simple alternative that gives you all the glory of ham without quite as much falderal.

:: **SERVES 12**

Spray the crock of a 7- to 8-quart slow cooker with baking spray.

Use a sharp knife to score a diamond pattern in the top of the ham, about 1 inch deep and ¼ inch apart. Place the ham in the slow cooker. Mix the mustard, honey, brown sugar, and bourbon together in a small bowl until smooth and pour over the ham. Cook on low for 3 to 4 hours, until the ham reaches an internal temperature of 140°F.

Remove the ham from the slow cooker and cover with foil. Let rest for 10 to 15 minutes before serving.

The ham can be served warm or at room temperature. It's excellent served with Sweet Hot Southern Mustard (see facing page).

1 (5-pound) boneless ham

½ cup Dijon mustard

½ cup honey

½ cup packed light brown sugar

¼ cup bourbon

SWEET HOT SOUTHERN MUSTARD

Perish the thought of store-bought mustard on a Southern buffet! As it happens, homemade mustard is easy to make, and can be tailored to suit any taste. Here I "Southern" it up with bourbon and sorghum, which go particularly well with hearty ham. Store the mustard and deliver it in mason jars, and serve it in a pretty silver bowl.

:: MAKES ABOUT 1½ PINTS

Set up a double boiler over medium-high heat. Place the ingredients in the carafe of a blender and blend until smooth. Pour the mustard mixture into the top of the double boiler and cook, stirring, until the mustard thickens, about 8 minutes. You want it just a little looser than sandwich-spreadable, as it will thicken as it cools and refrigerates. Cool the mustard in the pot off the heat, then pour it into a jar, cover, and refrigerate. Bring to room temperature before serving.

The mustard will keep covered in the refrigerator for a week.

3 eggs

1 (4-ounce) can yellow mustard powder

1 cup light brown sugar

1 cup cider vinegar

3 tablespoons bourbon

1 tablespoon sorghum syrup or molasses

The Ham

The majestic and marvelous ham is a staple of any Southern table, the crowning glory of a funeral spread. And it is a perfect food for the event, as it serves beautifully as a buffet dish, but always leaves plenty behind for the bereaved to eat in the gloomy days following. Sure, you can pick up a ham from a store, but preparing one yourself is a special tribute, and especially delicious. It takes a little time, but most of it is hands-off. Northern girl Dorothy Parker quipped that "eternity is two people and a ham," but most Southerners know that two people and a ham are just darn lucky.

COUNTRY HAM

Many of my most vivid childhood memories involve country ham (most of my lifetime memories involve food). My mother was born and raised in Columbia, Tennessee, in Maury County, in the middle of the state, and we visited my grandparents often, particularly for holidays and big events, and those events invariably featured a handsome country ham. It stayed wrapped in crinkled foil in the fridge until the big event, when it was unwrapped and placed proudly on a big silver tray and thinly sliced. The ham was served, in true Middle Tennessee style, with beaten biscuits, a lost culinary art. These little inch-round pucks are hard and flaky and crispy all at once. Few people make beaten biscuits anymore, as the laborious process involves beating the kneaded dough with a bat or thwapping it on a wooden counter top until the dough blisters, then running the mass through a biscuit brake, a device that looks like an instrument of torture but rolls the dough to an elastic, smooth sheet. The biscuits are then cut, precisely pricked with a fork, and baked until dry. When ready to eat, these magnificent biscuits may look like hard tack, but the slight twist of a butter knife slits one perfectly, so it's ready to receive a knob of butter and a slice of divine country ham.

In the process of planning this book, I knew that country ham had to play a role, so I goaded and cajoled my good friend Epps, who himself grew up in Maury County, to prepare a country ham in the old Columbia way, with an eye to recounting the recipe in these pages. Epps procured the ham from the town of Little Lot, very near Columbia, over Thanksgiving and decided to prepare it for his family's annual New Year's Eve party. We turned to the *James K. Polk Home Cookbook* from Columbia, to use the recipe printed there, from the undisputed expert in country ham preparation, Slick Moss, as Slick's Country Ham. I recount our adventure here.

Epps's attempts to remove the hock with a hand saw were unsuccessful, but in a stroke of good luck, he had just received a reciprocating saw for Christmas and put it to its first use. He soaked the ham overnight in water in one of those plastic, lidded storage bins, which I can only assume would never be storing the family's winter sweaters again. We were a little stymied when my largest water bath canner wasn't big enough for the ham—neither was my brother's fish fryer—so Epps scoured town for a pot large enough to boil the ham. I joined him for the official boiling, as he lowered the soaked ham into a huge pot set over an outdoor burner and filled it up with water. As per Slick's instructions, Epps had a large galvanized garbage can at the ready to nestle the ham in overnight. The original recipe calls for lining the garbage can with newspapers, but Epps had the ingenious idea to use an old sleeping bag instead. We cracked a couple of beers while the water came to a boil, then let the ham boil away for 45 minutes. I smartly made myself scarce for the complicated act of transferring the huge pot of ham and water to the sleeping bag–lined garbage can, where our baby rested overnight.

The next morning, I got the first in a series of texts and photos from Epps and his wife, Stephanie—the removal of the ham from the water (it's still hot!), the skin, which was slipped off, photographed for me and discarded. Epps coated the ham with a mixture of cracker crumbs and brown sugar and baked it slowly in the oven for several hours. Turns out, he has some real skill at carvery, and my modern electric knives were not required. Epps's mother made biscuits and brought the frozen dough to Memphis over Christmas, and the ham was nestled in these little gems and served to the New Year's Eve guests. My first bite transported me to holidays at my grandparents' house and I told my fellow diners and Epps that it was definitely the ham of my childhood. My brother sought me out at the party to exclaim over the sense memory. I had told my mother about the whole affair, and she told me to bring her some ham—if it was good. It was, indeed, good, and my mother echoed my exact words—"This is the ham of my childhood."

I told Epps that in my recounting of this tale, I would appear to be much more involved in the actual preparation, but I have to give credit where credit is due. At the party, we explained to everyone the story of the country ham and what a big part of our childhood the whole thing was. Several people asked if he would do it again—I think he will—and his comment was, maybe it would involve a little more drinking next time. Epps, I am totally down with that.

DEVILED HAM

If the devil has to make an appearance, this is the way to do it. It's a great way to use up a ham, but you can also make it from cooked ham slices bought from the deli.

:: MAKES ABOUT 2 CUPS

Place the ham, green onions, capers, chives, and thyme in the bowl of a food processor. Pulse until everything is very finely chopped. Add the cream cheese, mayonnaise, and mustard and pulse a few times to break up. Add the remaining ingredients and blend until thoroughly combined, scraping down the sides of the bowl as needed. Don't blend until completely smooth—you want a little bit of rough texture. Serve with crackers or as sandwich filling.

8 ounces cooked smoked ham, city or country

3 green onions

1 tablespoon capers

1 tablespoon roughly chopped chives

2 teaspoons thyme leaves

4 ounces cream cheese, softened

1/3 cup mayonnaise

1 tablespoon creole mustard (such as Zatarain's)

2 teaspoons Worcestershire sauce

1 teaspoon ground black pepper

1 teaspoon hot sauce

BAKED COUNTRY HAM AND CHEESE SANDWICHES

Ham, mustard, and poppy seed sandwiches have been a party staple all my life, usually made with the little yeast rolls sold in round tinfoil pans (and you can use this recipe that way as well). I'd seen pictures on the Internet of the Hawaiian roll version, so I made it that way for a book club event. A friend of Southern extraction who grew up in Utah immediately told me that these little bites were called "funeral sandwiches" when she was growing up, so I felt I must include them in the book. And they do make a wonderful funeral dish, as they are perfect for a buffet or can be kept in the fridge for a family to heat up for a quiet dinner. I've riffed on another community cookbook recipe to make a ham spread, which I think makes these easier to eat. Country ham gives a nice salty bite, but you could use regular smoked city ham.

:: MAKES 24 SANDWICHES

Line a 9-by-13-inch baking pan with foil, allowing it to hang over the edges—this makes it easier to lift out the cooked sandwiches. Use a high-sided brownie pan, not a shallower glass casserole.

Place the ham pieces and shallot in the bowl of a food processor fitted with the metal blade and pulse until everything is chopped very fine. Add the mustard and poppy seed and pulse until blended. Cut the softened butter into pieces and add to the bowl, then process to a smooth, well-combined paste.

Use a long, sharp bread knife to slice each package of rolls in half horizontally. Do not separate the individual rolls; slice open the whole rectangle. Spread the country ham mixture in an even layer over both of the bottom halves. I use a combination of a flexible spatula and my good, clean fingers to make sure the ham is spread evenly to the edges of the bread. Carefully transfer the covered pieces of bread to the prepared pan. They will fit snugly and you may have to wiggle them in and press them down. Toss

8 ounces center-cut country ham, cut into pieces

1 shallot, peeled and cut into pieces

2 tablespoons Dijon mustard

1 tablespoon poppy seeds

8 tablespoons (1 stick) unsalted butter, softened

2 packages (1 dozen each) soft Hawaiian rolls

4 ounces Swiss cheese, grated

4 ounces sharp Cheddar, grated

For the Topping:

8 tablespoons (1 stick) unsalted butter

¼ cup light brown sugar

2 tablespoons Dijon mustard

1 tablespoon poppy seeds

Melinda

Melinda was closing out the house after her father died, following her mother by several years. In a file cabinet drawer, she found all the important personal information and documents for each of her family members in individual files carefully marked with typewritten labels. Tucked between the file for her and one of her brothers was another folder, carefully labeled "Hams—Country". Inside, Melinda found a list of names that she was sure were the people her mother sent a country ham every year at Christmas. Yes, the country ham is very important in the South.

together the 2 grated cheeses and sprinkle an even layer over the ham filling, making sure to reach the edges of the bread. Place the top halves of the rolls over the cheese. Use a thin knife to run through the separations in the rolls to make them easier to pull apart when cooked.

FOR THE TOPPING:

Melt the butter, brown sugar, and mustard together in a small saucepan, then stir in the poppy seeds. When the butter is melted, bring the mixture to a boil and cook for 1 minute, stirring constantly. Drizzle the topping over the sandwiches in the pan, using a spatula to spread it out evenly, if needed. Leave to cool, then cover the pan with foil and refrigerate overnight.

When ready to cook, preheat the oven to 350°F. Bake the sandwiches, covered, for 30 minutes, until the cheese is melted and the sandwiches are heated through. Uncover and cook for a few minutes, just until the tops are lightly toasted—be careful, the topping can brown easily. Use the overhanging foil to lift the sandwiches from the pan, then separate them and arrange on a platter. These are lovely warm or at room temperature.

SLOW COOKER PULLED PORK WITH HOMEMADE BARBECUE SAUCE

As a born and bred Memphian, my blood runs part barbecue sauce. So, with the best barbecue in the world available 5 minutes from my house in every direction, I don't bother to smoke my own meat. But pulled pork shoulder is a wonderful thing to take to those in need of a comforting meal. Friends brought us a pork shoulder meal after my father's funeral and it was the perfect remedy. We absolutely devoured it.

This slow cooker recipe is a treat. For very little work, you get a delicious result that feeds a crowd. Pork shoulder will keep in the fridge for several days; it can be put on buns, over lettuce, or eaten straight up. I use a smoky version of my house barbecue spice and a homemade tangy sauce.

:: SERVES AT LEAST 8 AND MAKES ABOUT 2 CUPS SAUCE

FOR THE PORK:

Whisk all the spices and salts together in a small bowl, then sprinkle them all over the pork, pressing the rub into the sides of the meat. Place the sliced onions in the bottom of a 7- to 8-quart slow cooker and place the pork on top. Pour the beer into the bottom of the slow cooker. Cook until the meat is tender and falling apart, 5 hours on high or 8 hours on low. Lift the pork out of the slow cooker onto a rimmed baking dish and use two forks to shred the meat.

The pulled pork can be cooled, covered, and refrigerated for up to 3 days. Serve at room temperature, or heat at 350°F in a tightly

For the Pork:

1 tablespoon sweet paprika

1 tablespoon smoked paprika

1 teaspoon salt

1 teaspoon celery salt

1 teaspoon ground black pepper

½ teaspoon onion powder

½ teaspoon chile powder

½ teaspoon crushed red pepper

½ teaspoon garlic powder

¼ teaspoon cayenne

4 pounds boneless pork shoulder or Boston butt

1 onion, thinly sliced

1 cup beer

For the Sauce:

1¼ cup ketchup

1 cup dark brown sugar

¼ cup sorghum

¼ cup cider vinegar

¼ cup water

1 tablespoon Worcestershire sauce

2½ teaspoons ground mustard

2 teaspoons smoked paprika

1 teaspoon salt

½ teaspoon ground black pepper

½ teaspoon garlic powder

covered pan until just warm. The sauce can be stirred into the pork shoulder and reheated, or warmed in a saucepan and served on the side.

FOR THE SAUCE:

Combine all the ingredients in a saucepan and whisk to blend well. Bring to a boil over medium-high heat, then lower the heat and simmer until thickened, about 10 minutes, stirring frequently. The sauce can be covered and refrigerated for up to a week.

BEEF TENDERLOIN WITH HORSERADISH CREAM SAUCE

Beef Tenderloin is the true star of the Southern buffet, standing proudly on its silver platter sur-
rounded by parsley (curly, not flat leaf) and a dish and ladle of horseradish cream. It makes a most
elegant meal, but it also lends itself to being served with little dinner rolls to make bite-sized sand-
wiches for grazing.

:: SERVES 12 AND MAKES ABOUT 1½ CUPS SAUCE

FOR THE BEEF:

Pat the tenderloin dry with paper towels and place it on a platter. Mix the salt and peppers together in small bowl, then rub them all over every side of the meat. Place the meat in the fridge uncovered for at least an hour, but longer is better, up to a day.

Take the tenderloin out of the fridge an hour before cooking. Preheat the oven to 500°F. Place the meat in a roasting pan and cook for 20 minutes (that's 5 minutes per pound, if you need to adjust for size). Turn the oven off, but do not open the door. Leave the tenderloin in the oven for 2 hours. Put a sticky note on the oven door warning others not to open it!

Remove the tenderloin from the oven and let the meat rest for 15 minutes before slicing.

FOR THE SAUCE:

Beat the cream in the bowl of a stand mixer fitted with the whisk attachment until thick, but not holding stiff peaks. You want it to be almost the consistency of the sour cream. Beat in the sour cream, horseradish, lemon juice, mustard, and black pepper until well combined and smooth, scraping down the sides of the bowl a few times. Fold in the chives, then turn the cream out into a bowl. Cover with plastic wrap and refrigerate for at least an hour to allow the flavors to meld, but this will keep covered in the fridge for up to a week.

For the Beef:

1 (4-pound) beef tenderloin, trimmed and tied

2 tablespoons kosher salt

1 tablespoon ground black pepper

½ teaspoon white pepper

For the Sauce:

½ cup heavy whipping cream

½ cup sour cream

¼ cup prepared horseradish from a jar

1 tablespoon lemon juice

1 teaspoon Dijon mustard

Several grinds of black pepper

1 tablespoon finely snipped fresh chives

CUBAN PORK TENDERLOIN

Pork tenderloin is a perfect take-along, as it can be served warm or at room temperature. Serve it thinly sliced with little rolls, to make sandwiches, or in thicker slices for the dinner plate. I add a little flair to my tenders with a Cuban touch, which is just different enough from a traditional version to liven things up.

:: SERVES 20

Mix all the marinade ingredients in a large zip-top plastic bag. Add the pork to the marinade. Close the bag and turn the pork to coat. Refrigerate for several hours or overnight, turning the pork occasionally.

Preheat oven to 400°F. Transfer the pork to a baking pan; discard the marinade. Tuck any skinny ends underneath the tenderloin to ensure even cooking. Roast until a thermometer inserted into the center of the pork registers 145°F, about 25 minutes. Let the pork stand for 5 minutes. Cut it crosswise into ½-inch-thick slices. Serve warm or at room temperature.

½ cup fresh orange juice (about 1 medium orange)

¼ cup fresh lime juice (about 2 limes)

¼ cup dark rum

1 medium onion, thinly sliced

6 garlic cloves, minced

1 teaspoon ground cumin

1 teaspoon salt

1 bay leaf, crumbled

½ teaspoon ground black pepper

3 to 4 sprigs of thyme

2 (12-ounce) pork tenderloins

BARBECUE SPICED BRISKET

A friend made a version of this overnight brisket for book club and it was so good, everyone asked for the recipe. She told me it was a little embarrassing, because on the recipe card she had handed down from her mom, it was titled "funeral brisket"—but she likes it so much she makes it all the time. I've Memphis-ed it up with barbecue seasoning.

The low and slow cooking makes all the difference in creating a tender and flavorful brisket. I generally prepare the meat in the afternoon, then stick it in the oven overnight. In the morning, just transfer the meat to a platter and whir up the sauce.

:: SERVES 8

FOR THE RUB:

Mix all the spices and salts together in a small bowl and whisk to combine.

For the Rub:

2 tablespoons sweet paprika

1 teaspoon salt

1 teaspoon celery salt

1 teaspoon ground black pepper

½ teaspoon onion powder

½ teaspoon chili powder

½ teaspoon crushed red pepper

½ teaspoon garlic powder

½ teaspoon smoked paprika

¼ teaspoon cayenne

For the Brisket:

4 plum tomatoes

2 carrots

2 stalks celery

1 (3-pound) brisket

1 onion

FOR THE BRISKET:

Place three long pieces of foil in a 9-by-13-inch baking pan, in alternating directions. Cut the tomatoes in half and place them on the foil in the pan with the whole carrots and celery. Place the brisket on top, then sprinkle with the barbecue rub, coating the brisket completely with it. Flip the brisket over and coat the other side with spice mix. Slice the onion and separate into rings and spread over the top of the meat. Wrap the whole up in the foil creating a tight package. Refrigerate the brisket for several hours to let the spices permeate the meat.

When ready to cook, preheat the oven to 225°F and cook the meat for 8 hours. Remove the meat from the oven and unwrap the foil. Transfer the brisket to a platter to cool. Put the vegetables and cooking juices in a blender and blend until smooth. Pour this into a bowl, cool, cover, and refrigerate. Cool the brisket, and wrap it in foil and refrigerate for up to a day.

When ready to serve, preheat the oven to 425°F, unwrap the brisket and place it on a foil-lined baking dish. Spread ½ cup of the pureed vegetables over the top of the brisket and cook for 15 to 20 minutes, until the meat is heated through. Let the brisket rest for 15 minutes, then slice and serve. You can heat the pureed vegetables in a small saucepan with a little water to thin and serve it as a gravy for the brisket, if you'd like.

"They're going to put [him] in the window of his funeral home from 2 p.m. today. . . . Just last month [he] discussed why he had installed a drive-through window. 'A lot of people aren't comfortable coming into a funeral home,' he told the reporter, 'so when I designed the building, I wanted a window big enough so people could view the body from outside.'"

—*Obituary, Nashville Tennessee*

HOMEMADE BAKED SPAGHETTI

It's important not to forget kids in times of trouble. Funerals and visitations can be confusing and sad and momentous all at once. Lots of old people patting you on the head. And a parade of congealed salads and unfamiliar casseroles on the table are not exactly comforting to little ones. So here, I present a casserole that will please everyone with its sheer comfort. This is the one to sit down to as a family after all of the hullabaloo has quieted down.

:: SERVES 6 TO 8

FOR THE SAUCE:

Sauté the onions in the olive oil in a medium skillet over medium-high heat until they are soft and just beginning to brown. Add the garlic and sauté for a further minute, then pour in the wine. Bring the wine to a bubble and cook until it is almost completely evaporated, just a little glaze on the now purple onions. Pour in the tomatoes and stir well, then add the basil, oregano, sugar, salt, pepper, and nutmeg and stir well. Let simmer over medium-low heat for 5 minutes, then use an immersion blender to puree the sauce to a smooth consistency. Simmer for a further 5 minutes, then remove from the heat and cool. (Alternatively, you can simmer the sauce for the full 10 minutes, then puree it in a blender and leave to cool.)

The sauce can be made up to 2 days ahead, cooled, covered, and refrigerated.

FOR THE CASSEROLE:

Bring a large pot of salted water to the boil and cook the spaghetti 1 minute less than the package instructs, about 10 minutes. Drain the spaghetti and rinse with cool water.

Crumble the sausage into the pot and cook over medium-high heat, breaking up the meat with a spatula as it cooks. You want small pieces of sausage. When the sausage is no longer pink,

For the Sauce:

1 cup finely diced onion

2 tablespoons olive oil

4 cloves garlic, minced

½ cup red wine

1 (28-ounce) can crushed tomatoes

1 tablespoon chopped fresh basil

1 tablespoon chopped fresh oregano

2 teaspoons granulated sugar

1 teaspoon kosher salt

½ teaspoon ground black pepper

¼ teaspoon ground nutmeg

For the Casserole:

8 ounces spaghetti, broken in half

1 pound Italian sausage, bulk or links with the casing removed

1 (8-ounce) package cream cheese, at room temperature

1 cup whole cottage cheese

¼ cup sour cream

1 teaspoon chopped fresh basil

1 teaspoon chopped fresh oregano

Salt and ground black pepper, to taste

1 pound fresh mozzarella

Susan

When a relative of Susan's died in a very small town in Alabama, one of the local church ladies immediately volunteered to supply paper products for the visitation in the church basement, because, she exclaimed, she had a pantry full of them. What she brought included a big bag of folded paper napkins, printed with the cheerful logo of a regional fast food chain named Jack-in-the-Box. The deceased, unfortunately, was also named Jack.

drain off the accumulated fat and stir the meat into the tomato sauce.

Mix the cream cheese, cottage cheese, sour cream, and herbs together in a small bowl until thoroughly combined. Add salt and pepper to taste.

Spray a 9-by-13-inch baking dish with baking spray. Spread half the noodles on the bottom of the dish, then dollop over the cream cheese mixture. Spread it out into an even layer (you can use clean, damp hands if it helps). Top with the remaining noodles in an even layer, then spread the meat and tomato sauce evenly over the top.

Shred the mozzarella with your fingers into fine shreds over the top of the casserole, covering as much surface as you can. Cover the casserole with foil. At this point, the casserole can be cooled, covered, and refrigerated for 2 days.

When ready to serve, preheat the oven to 350°F and bake the casserole, covered, for 40 minutes. Remove the foil and cook a further 5 minutes. Let the casserole sit for 10 minutes before scooping into it to serve.

BAKED KIBBEH

Lebanese-style Baked Kibbeh may seem an odd thing to find in a book about Southern funerals, but not so. Throughout the Mississippi Delta and Arkansas, you'll find scattered pockets of families of Lebanese descent who've been there for generations. So traditional Lebanese dishes pop up in community cookbooks, on the steam table at meat-and-three restaurants, at football tailgates and state fairs. In fact, there's a kibbeh festival in Yazoo City, Mississippi. If that's not cross-cultural sharing, I don't know what is. I have an acquaintance from northern Mississippi who is of Lebanese descent, and every time I see her at parties we talk about food and we share recipes—my Hoppin' John for her tabouli. I asked her once for a kibbeh recipe and she told me, "Oh, I'm sure I must have it, but we only seem to make that for funerals anymore." I never got her recipe, but I assiduously researched both Southern recipes and Lebanese versions to create my own.

:: SERVES 8

FOR THE LEBANESE SPICE BLEND:

Whisk all the ingredients together in a small bowl until well blended.

FOR THE FILLING:

Heat the olive oil in a medium saucepan, then add the ground sirloin, breaking it into pieces. Add the onion, pine nuts, spice blend, and salt and cook, stirring and breaking up the meat until it is cooked through and the onion is soft and wilted. Remove from the heat and stir in the chopped mint. Leave to cool while you make the base.

FOR THE BASE:

Put the bulgur in a medium bowl and cover with water by about an inch. Leave to soak for 30 minutes. Make the filling while the bulgur soaks. Break the chuck up into a large mixing bowl, then add the onion, spice blend, mint, and salt. Knead together

For the Lebanese Spice Blend:

2 teaspoons ground black pepper

2 teaspoons ground cumin

2 teaspoons paprika

1 teaspoon ground coriander

1 teaspoon ground cloves

½ teaspoon ground nutmeg

½ teaspoon ground cinnamon

¼ teaspoon ground cardamom

For the Base:

1½ cups fine bulgur wheat

2 pounds ground beef chuck

1 cup grated onion (about ½ onion)

2 tablespoons Lebanese Spice Blend

1 tablespoon chopped fresh mint

1 teaspoon salt

2 tablespoons olive oil

For the Filling:

1 tablespoon olive oil

1 pound ground beef sirloin

1 cup grated onion (about ½ onion)

½ cup pine nuts

1 tablespoon Lebanese Spice Blend

1 teaspoon salt

1 tablespoon chopped fresh mint

with your good, clean hands, making sure everything is evenly distributed. Drain the bulgur through a clean tea towel set over a strainer. Squeeze out as much water as possible. Add the bulgur to the meat a cup at a time, kneading it in until all the bulgur is evenly mixed into the meat. Divide the mixture in half. Spray a 9-by-13-inch being dish with baking spray, then press half the mixture into an even layer over the bottom of the dish. Spread the cooled filling evenly over the base, and place handfuls of the remaining base evenly over the filling. Use lightly moistened hands to press the base into an even layer over the filling. Score a diamond pattern over the top of the kibbeh. Cover and refrigerate for up to a day.

When ready to bake the kibbeh, drizzle 2 tablespoons of olive oil over the top. Preheat the oven to 350°F. Bake the kibbeh until heated through, 30 to 40 minutes. Serve immediately.

Note: One large onion should produce enough grated onion—I prefer to grate the onion on the large holes of a box grater.

"When I die that ain't the time I'm going to start getting choosey. They can lay me in the nearest spot. When I pass from this world I'll be considerate of them that stay in it."

—Flannery O'Connor, *Judgement Day*

THE SWEET HEREAFTER

DESSERTS
AND SWEETS

JACK AND COKE SHEET CAKE

Rich chocolate cake, made moist with Co-cola (as we call it in the South) is only made better with a little toot of Tennessee's Jack Daniel's sour mash whiskey. What could be a better treat at a visitation?

:: SERVES 24

FOR THE CAKE:

Preheat the oven to 350°F. Spray an 18-by-12-inch sheet cake pan with baking spray.

Pour the Coke into a large saucepan and add the butter, cut into pieces, the cocoa powder, and the whiskey. Cook over medium heat, stirring frequently, until the butter is melted and the mixture is smooth. Whisk the flour, sugars, baking soda, and salt together in a large bowl until well combined. When the butter is melted, remove the pot from the heat and stir the cocoa mixture into the dry ingredients until completely blended and smooth. Measure the buttermilk into a 2-cup jug, then break in the eggs and add the vanilla. Beat the eggs with the buttermilk and vanilla, then add this to the batter and stir until it's completely combined. Spread the batter into the prepared pan in an even layer, all the way to the corners. Bake for 15 to 20 minutes, until a tester inserted in the center comes out clean. Make the frosting while the cake is in the oven.

FOR THE FROSTING:

Wipe out the pot and melt the butter with the Coke, whiskey, and cocoa powder over medium heat, stirring until combined. Beat in the confectioners' sugar about a cup at a time until the frosting is smooth and combined. Take the cake from the oven and pour the frosting over it, covering as much cake as possible. Tilt the cake pan or use a spatula to cover the entire surface, working quickly before the frosting begins to set. Leave the cake to cool. The cake can be made up to 2 days ahead and kept covered in a cool place.

For the Cake:

1 cup regular Coca-Cola

16 tablespoons (2 sticks) unsalted butter

¼ cup cocoa powder

2 tablespoons Jack Daniel's whiskey

2 cups all-purpose flour

1 cup light brown sugar, firmly packed

1 cup granulated sugar

1 teaspoon baking soda

½ teaspoon salt

½ cup whole buttermilk

2 eggs

1 teaspoon vanilla

For the Frosting:

14 tablespoons (1¾ sticks) unsalted butter

½ cup regular Coca-Cola

¼ cup Jack Daniel's whiskey

¼ cup cocoa powder

4 cups confectioners' sugar, sifted

STRAWBERRY BUTTERMILK SHEET CAKE

Strawberry cake is another Southern classic, the layered version being a favorite for wedding showers and ladies' birthdays. Many, many recipes for strawberry cake involve strawberry gelatin, boxed strawberry cake mix, frozen berries in syrup, or all of the above. However, I prefer mine made with fresh, in-season berries. This sheet cake version feeds a large crowd, so it's perfect for funeral gatherings. Buttermilk adds such tenderness and tang to baked goods, I use it whenever I can.

:: SERVES 24

FOR THE CAKE:

Preheat the oven to 350°F. Spray a 12-by-18-inch half sheet pan thoroughly with baking spray.

Puree the strawberries in the carafe of a blender until smooth. Pour 1 cup of the puree into a large mixing bowl (reserve ¼ cup for the frosting), then whisk in the eggs, melted and cooled butter, buttermilk, and vanilla until thoroughly combined. Stir in the sugar until combined, then add the flour, baking soda, and salt and fold into the batter until it is just mixed and there is no trace of the dry ingredients in the bowl. Scrape the batter into the prepared pan and spread out into an even layer. Bake for 20 minutes or until a tester inserted in the center of the cake comes out clean. Make the frosting while the cake is still warm.

FOR THE FROSTING:

Put the butter and the remaining ¼ cup strawberry puree in a large saucepan and heat on medium-high until the butter is melted. Stir in the buttermilk and bring to a boil. Remove the pan from the heat and beat in the confectioners' sugar a cup at a time, until you have a smooth frosting. If the icing is too thick to spread, beat in a little more strawberry puree or buttermilk, if

For the Cake:

1 pound strawberries, hulled

2 large eggs

16 tablespoons (2 sticks) unsalted butter, melted and cooled

½ cup whole buttermilk

1 teaspoon vanilla extract

2 cups granulated sugar

2 cups all-purpose flour

1 teaspoon baking soda

½ teaspoon kosher salt

For the Frosting:

12 tablespoons (1½ sticks) unsalted butter

¼ cup strawberry puree, reserved from the cake

2 tablespoons buttermilk

6 cups confectioners' sugar, sifted

Sweet Heavens

Behold the Southern sheet cake. Though the towering layered and frosted confections are often considered the pinnacle of the Southern hostess repertoire, Southerners like to feed, and feed big, at times of trouble and strife. So the large half-sheet pan cake is the perfect solution. It's even better when you can find inexpensive restaurant supply pans or the disposable tinfoil versions that come with their own protective tops— no need to worry about retrieving or returning the dish.

there is no puree left. Pour the frosting over the warm cake and spread it out in an even layer. An offset spatula is the best tool. Cool the cake completely.

Note: The cake does not bake up to a vivid pink like the one made with boxed ingredients. The icing will be nice and pink, but if you feel you need to, you can add a few drops of food coloring to the cake batter.

TENNESSEE SHEET CAKE

This is a classic worth repeating, easy to make, easy to carry, easy to keep—and easy to eat. The cake is marzipan-y with a sweet, sweet icing and it feeds a crowd. It may be known to some as White Texas Sheet Cake, but, hey, I'm from Tennessee.

:: **SERVES AT LEAST 24**

FOR THE CAKE:

Preheat the oven to 350°F. Spray a 12-by-18-inch half sheet pan with a baking spray.

In a large saucepan, heat the butter and water to boiling. While it is heating, stir together the eggs and sour cream in a bowl. Add the flour, sugar, almond extract, salt, and baking soda. Stir together as well as you can—it is stiff and won't completely mix. When the butter and water are boiling, remove from the heat and stir in the flour mixture, stirring until smooth. There may be a few lumps. Pour the batter into the prepared pan. Bake for 18 to 20 minutes until golden on the edges and a tester inserted in the middle comes out clean. Remove from the oven and leave to cool for 20 minutes.

FOR THE FROSTING:

When the cake is almost finished its 20-minute cooldown, prepare the frosting. Melt the butter in the milk in the cleaned saucepan and bring to a boil. Remove from the heat and stir in the confectioners' sugar and almond extract, until smooth. Stir in the pecan pieces. Spread the frosting over the top of the cake and leave to cool completely.

When completely cool, cover the top of the cake tightly with plastic wrap. The cake will keep for 2 days tightly covered on the counter.

For the Cake:

16 tablespoons (2 sticks) unsalted butter

1 cup water

2 eggs

½ cup sour cream

2 cups all-purpose flour

2 cups granulated sugar

1 teaspoon almond extract

1 teaspoon salt

1 teaspoon baking soda

For the Frosting:

8 tablespoons (1 stick) unsalted butter

½ cup milk

4½ cups confectioners' sugar

½ teaspoon almond extract

½ cup pecan pieces

DOUBLE CARAMEL BUNDT CAKE

The towering Southern caramel cake is a wonder to behold: fluffy white layers of tender cake thickly covered in decadent, sugary caramel icing. Alas, it is a skill I have not mastered. Getting the consistency of the icing just right is something for which I utterly lack the patience. But caramel cake is an important part of my family history. Special occasions have always called for caramel cake. And it is my beloved brother's favorite—what he always wants for his birthday. I have tried, and failed, many times to create such a cake. So I gave up and resorted to mail order. At some point, though, I realized that as a professional cook and recipe developer, I really ought to make my brother's birthday cake my own self. I finally created a glaze that is a perfect approximation of the classic cake frosting, a simple, foolproof glaze (and I am the fool who proves that it works). And the Bundt pan makes the cake easy for anyone. Here, I double down on the caramel flavor, with a rich brown sugar cake.

:: SERVES 10

FOR THE CAKE:

Preheat the oven to 325°F. Spray a 12-cup Bundt pan with a baking spray.

Beat the butter in the bowl of a stand mixer to break it up, then add the brown sugar and beat at medium-high until light and fluffy. Add the eggs, one at a time, beating well after each addition and scraping down the sides of the bowl. Beat in the flour, baking powder, and salt alternately with the cream, scraping down the sides of the bowl, until the batter is thoroughly combined and smooth. Beat on high for about 5 seconds, then scoop the batter into the prepared pan. Lightly wet your fingers and press the batter into an even layer.

For the Cake:

24 tablespoons (3 sticks) unsalted butter, at room temperature

3 cups packed light brown sugar

6 eggs, at room temperature

3 cups all-purpose flour

½ teaspoon baking powder

½ teaspoon kosher salt

1 cup heavy cream

For the Glaze:

4 tablespoons (½ stick) unsalted butter

½ cup packed light brown sugar

⅓ cup heavy cream

¼ teaspoon kosher salt

1 cup confectioners' sugar, sifted

Bake the cake for 1 hour 20 minutes or until a tester inserted in the center comes out clean. Cool in the pan for 15 minutes, then invert onto a cooling rack set over a piece of waxed paper or foil. Cool completely.

FOR THE GLAZE:

The cake must be completely cool or the glaze will slide right off. The piece of foil or paper under the cooling rack will catch any drips and make cleanup easier.

Cut the butter into cubes and place in a large saucepan with the brown sugar, cream, and salt. After everything melts together, bring to a full rolling boil over medium heat, stirring constantly. When it reaches that boil, count to 60 Mississippi, then pull the saucepan off the heat. Leave the pan to cool for about 3 minutes, then vigorously beat in the confectioners' sugar until smooth.

Immediately pour the glaze over the cake, but do so slowly and evenly in order to cover as much surface as possible. Leave the glaze to set, then slice and enjoy. Covered tightly, this cake will last a few days.

"Nobody in the world eats better than the bereaved Southerner."

—Gayden Metcalfe and Charlotte Hays,

Being Dead Is No Excuse

COCONUT BUNDT CAKE

I am simply not patient enough to make the beauteous Southern coconut cake that reigns supreme on the shared spread. Layer cakes are not my specialty, and the really traditional method of cracking and grating a fresh coconut is beyond my patience level. Hence this cake—which is packed with coconut flavor, easy to make and serves plenty of folks. I carefully press lots of coconut into the glaze to give it that ethereal, fluffy look of its layered cousin.

:: **SERVES 12**

FOR THE CAKE:

Preheat the oven to 350°F. Spray a 12-cup Bundt pan with baking spray.

Stir the flour, baking powder, and salt together in a small bowl.

Beat the butter in the bowl of a stand mixer fitted with the paddle attachment to break it up, then add the sugar and beat until light and fluffy. Beat in the vanilla, then add the eggs, one at a time, beating well after each addition and scraping down the sides of the bowl a few times. Stir the coconut milk to blend any solids, then beat into the batter. Beat in the dry ingredients until well combined, scraping the bowl a few times. Sprinkle over the coconut and beat to distribute evenly, then beat the batter on high for 5 seconds. Scrape the beater and stir any clinging coconut shreds into the batter, then spread it into the prepared pan. Bake for 50 minutes to an hour, until a tester inserted in the center comes out clean.

Cool for 5 minutes in the pan, then turn out onto a wire rack to cool completely. Place a piece of parchment or foil under the rack to catch drips when you glaze the cake to make cleanup easy.

For the Cake:

2½ cups all-purpose flour

2 teaspoons baking powder

½ teaspoon salt

16 tablespoons (2 sticks) unsalted butter, at room temperature

2½ cups granulated sugar

1 teaspoon vanilla extract

6 large eggs

1 cup unsweetened coconut milk

½ cup shredded sweetened coconut

For the Glaze:

2 cups confectioners' sugar

6 to 8 tablespoons unsweetened coconut milk

2 cups sweetened shredded coconut

FOR THE GLAZE:

Sift the confectioners' sugar into a bowl and whisk in the coconut milk until you have a thick, spreadable glaze. Use a spoon to drizzle and spread the glaze over the top and down the sides of the cake. As you drizzle, cover the glaze with the shredded coconut, lightly pressing it into the glaze with clean fingers. You want a generous layer of coconut on the top and some coconut on the sides of the cake. Leave the cake uncovered for a few hours to let the glaze and coconut set.

The cake will keep, covered with plastic wrap, for 2 days.

PINEAPPLE UPSIDE DOWN BUNDT CAKE

Pretty, and maybe a little silly, this sweet cake looks lovely on a cake stand at the buffet and is packed with old-school comfort.

:: SERVES 10

Preheat oven to 350°F. Spray a 12-cup Bundt pan with baking spray.

Drain the pineapple through a sieve over a small bowl or measuring cup, pressing out as much juice as possible. Reserve the juice.

Melt 2 tablespoons of butter in a small saucepan over medium heat. Stir in the light brown sugar and 2 tablespoons of the drained pineapple juice and bring to a boil. Boil for 1 minute, then remove from the heat and stir in the drained pineapple. Spread the pineapple mixture in an even layer over the bottom of the prepared pan. Drain the cherries and press a cherry into each indentation of the Bundt pan in a decorative manner.

Beat the remaining 12 tablespoons of softened butter in the bowl of a stand mixer to break it up, then add the granulated sugar and beat until fluffy and pale, scraping down the sides of the bowl as needed. Add the eggs one at a time, beating well after each addition and scraping the bowl. Beat in the vanilla. Measure 1/3 cup of the reserved pineapple juice and add the milk to it. Beat in the flour, baking powder, and salt into the butter mixture alternately with the juice and milk, in two additions. When everything is well combined, beat the batter on high for about 5 seconds.

Dollop the batter carefully over the pineapples and cherries in the pan—you don't want to disturb the cherries. When you've got all the batter evenly dolloped in the pan, lightly wet your fingers and press the batter into an even layer.

1 (20-ounce) can crushed pineapple

16 tablespoons (2 sticks) unsalted butter, divided and softened

2 tablespoons light brown sugar, packed

About 14 maraschino cherries

1 1/3 cups granulated sugar

2 large eggs

1 teaspoon vanilla

1/3 cup whole milk

2 cups all-purpose flour

2 teaspoons baking powder

1/2 teaspoon salt

Bake the cake for 45 minutes, until a tester inserted in the center comes out clean. Cool the cake in the pan for 15 minutes, then invert it onto a platter. Leave the pan upside down on the platter for a few minutes, then carefully lift it from the cake. If some pineapple has stuck to the pan leaving gaps in the cake, just scrape it out and press it into the cake. Leave to cool completely before slicing and serving. The cake will keep for a day well-covered.

"Authorities say that the brother of [the deceased] . . . who was killed . . . last month, got into an argument with his father over an obituary written for the funeral. According to the grandfather, the brother's name was left out."

—Obituary, Baltimore, Maryland

BROWN SUGAR ANGEL FOOD CAKE

Angel Food Cake seems a perfectly obvious dessert to take to a funeral. Depending on the deceased, it may be the only angel in the room! I prefer this version made with brown sugar for its deeper, richer taste.

:: **SERVES 12**

Put the egg whites into the bowl of a stand mixer and let sit at room temperature for 30 minutes. Sift the flour into a large bowl. Sift ½ cup of brown sugar into a small bowl, then sift the remaining 1 cup of brown sugar into the flour. I simply push the brown sugar through a sieve with a flexible spatula to break up any lumps. Stir the flour and sugar together with a fork, breaking up any lumps.

1½ cups egg whites (from about 10 eggs)

1 cup cake flour

1½ cups light brown sugar

2 teaspoons vanilla extract

1½ teaspoons cream of tartar

½ teaspoon kosher salt

Elizabeth

Not long after Elizabeth got married, many decades ago, she moved to a small town with her husband, a place from which neither of them originated. As a young bride, she was eager to befriend the ladies of the town. And her first opportunity was at the funeral of the man who had founded the business where her husband had just taken the job that precipitated their move. So she pulled out her standby family recipe, the cake her mother had taught her to make that had always impressed her friends—and even her in-laws. She knew it was a surefire hit. And sure enough, in the church hall, people were helping themselves to slices of her cake and complimenting her. One older lady asked her for the recipe and Elizabeth proudly exclaimed, "It's my grandmother's rum cake." The room went silent, plates were set down. Finally, another town transplant pulled Elizabeth aside to explain that this congregation, the deceased gentleman, the company, and in fact most of the town, were stridently teetotal. Shortly thereafter, Elizabeth bought *The Joy of Cooking* and learned to make a chocolate cake.

Preheat the oven to 350°F. Fit the whisk attachment to a mixer and add the ½ cup of brown sugar to the egg whites in the bowl. Beat on medium speed until everything is foamy, about 3 minutes. Add the vanilla, cream of tartar, and salt to the whites and beat on high speed until the whites hold stiff peaks, scraping down the sides of the bowl a few times. When you lift the beaters, the whites should stand straight up and not flop over at all. Take the bowl off the mixer and gradually and gently fold in the flour and brown sugar mixture until everything is thoroughly combined and no dry ingredients are left. Use a spatula to gently fold the egg whites over the dry ingredients, making sure not to stir or knock the volume out of the airy whites.

Evenly scrape the batter into an ungreased angel food cake pan. Run the edge of the spatula in a channel through the center of the batter to prevent air bubbles, then bake the cake for 40 to 50 minutes, until the top is golden brown, appears dry and is no longer glossy, even in any cracks that form on the surface. A tester inserted in the center should come out clean. Immediately invert the cake over a wire rack and leave to cool completely, about 1 hour. Run a knife around the edge of the pan and around the center tube, then remove the sides of the pan. Run the knife between the cake and the bottom of the pan, then remove the cake to a platter.

Covered well, this cake will keep for several days.

Note: I happily use liquid egg whites bought in the carton to make things easier and quicker. If you separate your own eggs, make sure there is absolutely no yolk in with the whites or they will not beat to stiff peaks.

VANILLA BEAN BUTTER CAKE

I served this cake to my extended family after one of my recipe tests, and one of the gentlemen at the table declared it "the perfect cake." For him, it was everything he likes in a dessert—light, tender and not overly sweet, and very simple. He even packed up the leftovers to take to a visitation the next morning.

:: SERVES 12

FOR THE CAKE:

Preheat the oven to 350°F. Spray a 10-inch tube pan with baking spray.

Beat the butter in the bowl of a stand mixer fitted with the paddle attachment to loosen it up, then beat in the sugar until light and fluffy, about 5 minutes, scraping down the sides of the bowl as needed. Scrape the seeds from the vanilla bean and add to the butter with the vanilla extract, and beat until evenly distributed. Beat the eggs in one at a time, beating well after each addition and scraping down the sides of the bowl as needed.

Mix the flour, baking powder, baking soda, and salt together in small bowl. Add this to the batter in three additions, alternating with the buttermilk, beating on a medium-low speed and scraping down the sides of the bowl as needed. Spread the batter evenly in the prepared pan.

Bake the cake for 50 to 60 minutes until a tester inserted in the center comes out clean.

Take the cake from the oven and run a skewer or thin knife around the edges to loosen the cake. Leave to cool slightly while you make the butter glaze.

For the Cake:

16 tablespoons (2 sticks) unsalted butter, at room temperature

2 cups granulated sugar

1 vanilla bean

2 teaspoons vanilla extract

4 large eggs

3 cups all-purpose flour

1 teaspoon baking powder

½ teaspoon baking soda

½ teaspoon kosher salt

1 cup buttermilk

For the Butter Glaze:

8 tablespoons (1 stick) unsalted butter

1 cup granulated sugar

¼ cup water

2 teaspoons vanilla extract

Scraped vanilla pod

The Second Line

On almost any New Orleans
weekend, you can track down
a Second Line parade. Local
brass bands and dancers
march and strut through
neighborhoods in a raucous
tribute to the long history
of New Orleans music and
community. But the origins of
the Second Line are traditional
New Orleans funerals, in
which they still play an
important role.

With deep roots in the
African-American community,
West African tradition, and
the early military history
of New Orleans, funeral
processions have been a staple
of the city for centuries. The
musicians and the family of
the deceased are considered
the main line, and all the rest
of the mourners form the
second line. Somber music
and hymns would be played
to escort the body to the
cemetery, while up-tempo
music accompanied the trip
home. The solemn march
transforms into a celebration
of life, complete with dancing,
singing, whistles, cowbells,
and tambourines, as the body
is "cut loose" from the world.

FOR THE BUTTER GLAZE:

Put a piece of waxed or parchment paper under a cooling rack on
the counter to catch drips. Cut the butter into small pieces and
put these in a small pan with the sugar, water, vanilla extract,
and the vanilla pod. Heat over medium heat, stirring frequently,
until the butter is melted and the sugar is dissolved and no longer
granular. Poke holes all over the surface of the cake with a skewer
or toothpick, then spoon about a quarter of the butter glaze
evenly over the top. Let the glaze soak in for 5 minutes, then invert the cake out onto the rack. Poke holes all over the cake again,
then spoon over the next quarter of the glaze and leave it to soak
in for 5 minutes. Spoon over the next bit of glaze, and brush some
over the sides of the cake with a pastry brush. Leave to soak in
for 5 more minutes, then spoon and brush the last of the glaze all
over the cake. Leave to cool completely.

TRADITIONAL POUND CAKE

A simple pound cake is the most satisfying and comforting food gifts I know. Its appeal is broad and it offers scope, to be served plain or with ice cream, a sauce, or berries. It makes a dessert, a snack, and frankly, a very good breakfast. For most of my life, I honestly did not know that the name "pound cake" comes from the original ingredients—a pound of each. As I got more interested in cooking and learning about recipes and where they came from, I had to give the traditional pound cake a try. This is a distillation of all my experiments over the years—tips from friends, and recipes old and new. So here is my breakdown on how to make a great pound cake.

I have read some theories that the traditional pound cake recipe went out of fashion because it made too much cake (no such thing, in my opinion). I do scoff at that idea, because a well-wrapped pound cake keeps on the counter for days, even improves. Lightly toasting a slice brings a drying cake to life. And a cake wrapped tightly in plastic wrap and then foil freezes beautifully. The ingredients are so few and simple, so I really like to use the best I can—European style butter and farm fresh local eggs.

:: MAKES 2 LOAVES

Let the butter and the eggs come to room temperature.

Butter two 9-by-5-inch loaf pans. I like the Pyrex or tempered glass version, because you get a lighter crust and you can see what's going on. The wrappers that the butter softened in are a great tool for buttering the pans.

Put the butter into the bowl of a stand mixer fitted with the paddle attachment and beat it on medium for 1 minute until it starts to look lighter. Weigh the sugar in a bowl and pour it slowly into the butter with the mixer running. Beat the butter and sugar together at medium for 6 minutes, stopping to scrape down the sides of the bowl a couple of times. The butter will become super light and fluffy and almost white.

Break the eggs into a small bowl and whisk lightly. Weigh the flour in a small bowl (use the same one you used for the sugar). Turn the mixer to low and add the eggs and the flour alternately in three additions, beating well after each addition. Stop to scrape the bowl a few times. Add the vanilla or almond extract with the last addition of eggs, if using.

1 pound (4 sticks) unsalted butter (the best quality you can manage)

1 pound granulated sugar (about 2 cups)

1 pound eggs (about 8 medium or 7 large)

1 pound all-purpose flour (about 3¼ cups)

1 teaspoon vanilla extract or ¼ teaspoon almond extract (optional)

Divide the batter between the prepared pans. Smooth the batter to fill the pan, but don't worry about perfection. Place the pans on the middle rack of a cold oven, and turn it on to 275°F. Bake for 30 minutes, then rotate the pans and turn the temperature to 350°F. Bake an additional 15 to 25 minutes, until a tester inserted in the center comes out with a few clinging crumbs. If the tops of the cakes are getting too brown, loosely place a piece of tinfoil over the pans.

Cool the cakes on a wire rack in the pans for 15 minutes, then remove from the pans to the rack to finish cooling.

BOURBON BROWN BUTTER PECAN PIE

The queen of Southern pies—no gathering would be complete without a pecan pie. Most cooks have a favorite version, and I would never suggest that your family's is not the best ever—but I take the classic up a notch with toasted pecans, a shot of bourbon, and rich, nutty browned butter.

:: SERVES 6

FOR THE CRUST:

Place the flour, salt, and sugar in the bowl of a food processor and pulse a few times to mix. Drop in the small pieces of cold butter and pulse several times until the mixture is crumbly, but some minute pieces of butter are still visible. Sprinkle the water over, a tablespoon at a time, and pulse to combine. When the pastry just comes together, dump the dough onto a lightly floured surface and pat into a disk about ¾ inch thick. Wrap the disk in plastic wrap and refrigerate for at least 1 hour before rolling.

When ready to roll, place the disk on a lightly floured surface and, using a floured rolling pin, roll out the pastry to a round about 14 inches in diameter, to fit a 9-inch pie plate. Carefully drape the pastry over the rolling pin and transfer to the pie dish. Gently fit into the bottom and sides of the dish. Trim any overhanging pastry and lightly dust the bottom of the prepared crust with flour. Set aside.

FOR THE FILLING:

Preheat the oven to 425°F.

Cut the butter into small pieces and place in a small saucepan over medium heat. Cook the butter, swirling the pan occasionally, until the foam begins to subside and the butter is a nice toasty brown and smells nutty. Pour it into a measuring cup or small bowl and leave to cool (if you leave it in the hot pan it will continue to cook and will burn).

Place the chopped pecans in a large, dry skillet and toast over medium-high heat, just until the nuts begin to toast and release their lovely, nutty fragrance. Set aside to cool.

For the Crust:

1¼ cups all-purpose flour

½ teaspoon salt

½ teaspoon granulated sugar

8 tablespoons (1 stick) cold unsalted butter, cut into small pieces

2 to 4 tablespoons ice water

For the Filling:

8 tablespoons (1 stick) unsalted butter

1½ cups chopped pecans

4 large eggs

1 cup cane syrup

½ cup granulated sugar

2 tablespoons bourbon

Pinch of kosher salt

Beat the eggs in a mixing bowl, then beat in the cane syrup, sugar, bourbon, and salt. Stir in the cooled brown butter, leaving any residue in the measuring cup, then add the cooled pecans. Pour the filling into the prepared crust making sure the nuts are evenly distributed. Carefully transfer to the oven and cook 40 to 50 minutes, until the center is puffed up and no longer wobbly. I recommend that you shield the edges of the crust with foil or a crust shield before the pie goes in the oven. It is hard to do when the pie is hot. Remove the cooked pie from the oven and leave to cool completely. The pie will keep wrapped tightly for 2 days, or can be wrapped in plastic wrap, then foil, and frozen for up to 6 months.

Note: I think chopped pecans make the pie easier to eat, but if you prefer traditional pecan halves, feel free to use them.

"[She] passed away surrounded by her children, grandchildren and loved ones watching her favorite movie, A Christmas Story. *She immediately announced her departure from this Earth with a single thunderclap and a few moments of rain. The entire house went black as the power went out for several minutes. Two minutes later, the power returned. We knew [she] was announcing her arrival home!"*

—*Obituary, Memphis, Tennessee*

BUTTERMILK PIE BARS

Buttermilk pie is a particular favorite of mine. Simple, creamy, tangy, and sweet, you really can't go wrong with the classic. This version keeps all the traditional flavor, but serves a crowd in convenient bar form.

:: MAKES 15 BARS

FOR THE CRUST:

Preheat the oven to 350°F. Line a 9-by-13-inch baking pan with foil or parchment paper.

Place 2 cups of the flour, the confectioners' sugar, the butter, and the salt in the bowl of a stand mixer fitted with the paddle attachment and blend until combined but crumbly. Scatter the crumbs in the bottom of the prepared pan and press evenly into a uniform crust. Bake for 20 minutes until firm and golden in places.

FOR THE FILLING:

Clean out the mixer bowl and beater, then crack in the eggs, add the buttermilk and sugar, and beat until combined. Add the melted butter, vanilla, cornstarch, and nutmeg and beat until smooth and thoroughly combined. Pour the filling over the crust and spread to completely cover the crust. Bake for 30 to 35 minutes, until golden around the edges and firm.

Cool completely. The entire block, before slicing, can be wrapped and refrigerated for a day. Slice into squares for serving.

For the Crust:

2 cups all-purpose flour

½ cup confectioners' sugar

16 tablespoons (2 sticks) unsalted butter, softened

½ teaspoon kosher salt

For the Filling:

3 large eggs

1½ cups whole buttermilk

1 cup granulated sugar

8 tablespoons (1 stick) unsalted butter, melted and cooled

2 teaspoons vanilla extract

1½ teaspoons cornstarch

¼ teaspoon nutmeg

COLUMBIA CHESS PIE

Chess pie is definitely at the top of my personal list of comfort foods. Simple, sweet and satisfying, this classic Southern dessert holds lots of memories from my childhood visits to my grandparents in Columbia, Tennessee. This recipe is my grandmother's—but she frequently made it as little individual pies.

:: SERVES 6

FOR THE CRUST:

Place the flour, salt, and sugar in the bowl of a food processor and pulse a few times to mix. Drop in the small pieces of cold butter and pulse several times until the mixture is crumbly, but some minute pieces of butter are still visible. Sprinkle the water over, a tablespoon at a time, and pulse to combine. When the pastry just comes together, dump the dough onto a lightly floured surface and pat into a disk about ¾ inch thick. Wrap the disk in plastic wrap and refrigerate for at least 1 hour before rolling.

When ready to roll, place the disk on a lightly floured surface and, using a floured rolling pin, roll out the pastry to a round about 14 inches in diameter, to fit a 9-inch pie plate. Carefully drape the pastry over the rolling pin and transfer to the pie dish. Gently fit into the bottom and sides of the dish. Trim any overhanging pastry. Set aside.

FOR THE FILLING:

Preheat the oven to 350°F.

Whisk the sugar, cornmeal, flour, and salt together in a medium bowl. Lightly beat the eggs in a large bowl, then add the butter, milk, vinegar, and vanilla and stir to combine. Add the dry ingredients and stir until everything is thoroughly combined and no dry ingredients are visible in the mix. Pour into the pie crust. Carefully transfer to the oven and cook 40 to 50 minutes until the center is puffed up and no longer wobbly. I recommend that you shield the edges of the crust with foil or a crust shield before the pie goes in the oven. It is hard to do when the pie is hot. Leave to cool completely. The pie will keep wrapped in foil for 2 days.

For the Crust:

1¼ cups all-purpose flour

½ teaspoon salt

½ teaspoon granulated sugar

8 tablespoons (1 stick) cold unsalted butter, cut into small pieces

2 to 4 tablespoons ice water

For the Filling:

2 cups granulated sugar

2 tablespoons cornmeal

1 tablespoon all-purpose flour

¼ teaspoon kosher salt

4 large eggs

8 tablespoons (1 stick) unsalted butter, melted and cooled

¼ cup whole milk or buttermilk

1 tablespoon white vinegar

½ teaspoon vanilla extract

BANANA PUDDING, FOSTER'S STYLE

Banana pudding is for some members of my family the queen of desserts. I've always thought it was invented as a use for the glass or crystal trifle bowl so many Southern women have tucked away in the back of a cabinet.

:: SERVES 8

FOR THE PUDDING:

Pour the milk into a large, deep saucepan and heat over medium just until warm to the touch and little bubbles appear on the surface. While the milk is heating, beat the eggs in the bowl of a stand mixer fitted with the paddle attachment until creamy; then beat in the sugars, flour, and vanilla, scraping the sides and bottom of the bowl. Beat in 1½ cups of the warm milk until fully combined, then scrape the mixture back into the saucepan with the remaining milk. Heat over medium, stirring constantly, until the pudding has thickened—just a bit thinner than pudding should be as it will thicken on cooling. Pour the pudding through a sieve into a bowl, then place a piece of plastic wrap directly on the surface of the pudding. Refrigerate for 1 hour.

FOR THE BANANAS:

Melt the butter with the sugar and rum in a large saucepan. Bring to a boil, stirring constantly, and cook for 3 minutes. Reduce the heat and cook a further 3 minutes until the syrup is slightly thickened. Slice the bananas into ½-inch-thick pieces and drop them into the syrup. Stir gently to coat the bananas in the syrup and cook until warmed through.

For the Pudding:

6 cups milk

3 large eggs

1½ cups light brown sugar, packed

½ cup granulated sugar

¾ cup all-purpose flour

2 teaspoons vanilla extract

For the Bananas:

8 tablespoons (1 stick) unsalted butter

½ cup light brown sugar

½ cup dark rum

1 teaspoon vanilla

6 bananas

Assembly:

2 (10-ounce) boxes shortbread cookies, such as Lorna Doones, or vanilla wafers

TO ASSEMBLE:

Make a layer of half the cookies in the bottom of 3-quart glass trifle bowl or dish. Spoon over an even layer of bananas and syrup, then a half of the pudding. Layer over the remaining cookies, then the bananas, and finish with a layer of pudding, spreading it evenly to cover the bananas. Leave to cool, then cover with plastic wrap and refrigerate for at least 4 hours, but overnight is fine.

KENTUCKY BOURBON BALLS

Little bites of bourbon can't be anything but a welcome treat during a sad time—no one has to know you are having a little nip. My version of the candy classic tastes just enough of delicious bourbon without it feeling like you've done a shot when you pop it in your mouth. A little sorghum syrup brings out the earthiness of the pecans and bourbon. For a true indulgence, I like to dip these in milk chocolate, but you can use bittersweet for a more sophisticated edge, or a combo of both.

:: MAKES ABOUT 25 BOURBON BALLS

Toast the pecans in a dry skillet, just until they are fragrant and lightly golden. Don't let them get too dark or burn. Transfer immediately to an airtight jar or container and pour over the

1¼ cup pecan halves

6 tablespoons bourbon

8 tablespoons (1 stick) unsalted butter, softened

1 (1-pound) box confectioners' sugar

1 teaspoon vanilla extract

1 tablespoon sorghum syrup

1 pound, 2 ounces milk chocolate chips

bourbon. Leave to cool, then seal the jar and shake to coat the pecans in bourbon. Leave to soak for 24 hours, shaking the jar around if you happen to pass it.

When the pecans have had a good soak, drain the liquid off and place the nuts in the bowl of a small food processor. Pulse to very finely chop the pecans, but don't let them turn into a paste. Set aside.

Beat the butter in the bowl of a stand mixer fitted with the paddle attachment on medium-high to break it up. Reduce the speed to low and add the confectioners' sugar. Beat for about 3 minutes, scraping down the sides and the bottom of the bowl, until everything starts to come together. It may look like it never will, but make sure to scrape the butter from the bowl and increase the mixer speed as the sugar blends in. Beat in the vanilla extract, then drizzle in the sorghum and beat for another minute. Add the chopped pecans and beat until it all comes together in a ball, a total beating time of about 6 minutes. You want to be able to roll the filling into balls, so beat it well until it all comes right.

Roll tablespoons of the filling into balls and place on a waxed paper–lined baking sheet or platter. Freeze until firm and very cold, about 1 hour.

Melt the chocolate in a small, deep saucepan over low heat, stirring frequently, or in a small bowl in the microwave, until completely melted and smooth. A small, deep vessel makes dipping the balls easier. Remove the chocolate from the heat and drop the balls in one at a time and roll them around with a fork to coat. Remove them with the fork, allowing excess chocolate to drip back into the pot. Place each coated ball back on the baking sheet, making sure they do not touch, and repeat until all the balls are coated. If the chocolate begins to harden or seize, just return it to low heat and stir until it smooths out and continue coating the candy. Leave the balls to harden for several hours, then transfer them to a covered container.

The balls will keep in an airtight container for a week.

DIVINITY

I simply don't think you could write a book about funeral food without including a recipe with the utterly apropos name Divinity. I love Divinity—someone used to give it to my grandparents for Christmas and I would sneak pieces—but it has taken me to this point in my life to tackle making it myself. Turns out, it isn't difficult, it just takes patience and planning. Have all your tools and ingredients prepped and ready to go before you start, and do not look away during the process.

:: MAKES ABOUT 25 PIECES OF CANDY

2 cups granulated sugar

½ cup light corn syrup

½ cup hot water

2 egg whites

1 teaspoon vanilla extract

½ cup finely chopped pecans

Stir the sugar, corn syrup, and water together in a heavy medium saucepan, preferably one with a pouring spout. Fit a candy thermometer to the side of the pan. Place your stand mixer as close to the stove as you can and fit it with the whisk attachment. Line two baking sheets with waxed paper and place them near the mixer. Place the egg whites in the bowl of the mixer, measure out the vanilla extract and pecans, and have them close to hand. Place two tablespoons nearby ready for work.

Cook the sugar mixture over medium-high heat, stirring until the sugar is dissolved. Once it is dissolved, do not stir anymore. Heat the sugar to 250°F (the hard-ball stage). This takes about 5 minutes after the sugar has dissolved. While the sugar is cooking, beat the egg whites on high speed until they hold stiff peaks. Lift up the beater and a nice peak of white should stand straight and tall and not flop over.

When the sugar reaches temperature, turn the mixer onto high and slowly drizzle the hot syrup into the whites. Do not stop the mixer. Beat for about 2 minutes, then add the vanilla extract. Continue beating until the mixture is thick and loses its glossy sheen, about 6 more minutes (for a total of 8 minutes). When you lift the beater at this point, the mixture should fall in a ribbon that mounds back on itself in the bowl. Beat in the pecans.

Working quickly, scoop a tablespoon full of the mixture out of the bowl and use the other spoon to scrape it into a mound on the prepared waxed paper pan. If the first attempt spreads and flattens out, beat the candy for another minute, then start fresh.

If the mixture become too stiff to work with, turn the beater on and slowly drizzle in a little hot water to loosen it up. When you've scooped out all the candy, move the baking sheets to an out-of-the-way counter and leave the candy to harden and set for several hours (up to 12), then transfer to an airtight container for up to a week.

INDEX

PHOTO CREDITS

Page 13: © Redphotographer/iStockPhoto.com; page 19: © Diane Labombarbe/iStockPhoto.com; pages 21, 47: © photokitchen/iStockPhoto.com; page 25: © Bildagentur Zoonar GmbH/Shutterstock.com; page 26: © Elzbieta Sekowska/Shutterstock.com; page 30: © rudisill/iStockPhoto.com; page 35: © rjgrant /iStockPhoto.com; page 39: © Malkovstock/iStockPhoto.com; page 41: © Chalermsak/Shutterstock .com; page 42: © vaivirga/Shutterstock.com; page 48: © JoannaTkaczuk/Shutterstock.com; page 54: © NicolasMcComber/iStockPhoto.com; pages 57, 95, 122: © bhofack2/iStockPhoto.com; page 64: © DelaLane Photography/Shutterstock.com; page 67: © Rouzes/iStockPhoto.com; page 69: © stuartpitkin /iStockPhoto.com; page 70: © KabordaM/iStockPhoto.com; page 72: © gosphotodesign/Shutterstock. com; page 73: © Cheryl E. Davis/Shutterstock.com; page 74: © 1MoreCreative/iStockPhoto.com; page 77: © man_kukuku/Shutterstock.com; page 80: © KathyDewar/iStockPhoto.com; page 82: © Creative-Family /iStockPhoto.com; page 85: © Lilechka75/iStockPhoto.com; page 87: © -lvinst-/iStockPhoto.com; page 96: © MSPhotographic/iStockPhoto.com; page 103: © ivandzyuba/iStockPhoto.com; page 105: © ginauf /iStockPhoto.com; page 109: © Paul_Brighton/Shutterstock.com; page 114: © LauriPatterson/iStockPhoto .com; page 125: © Joe Gough/Shutterstock.com; page 127: © Brent Hofacker/Shutterstock.com; page 128: © farbled/Shutterstock.com; page 131: © Mariha-kitchen/iStockPhoto.com; page 137: © Marta Ortiz/iStock Photo.com; page 142: © Josie Grant/Shutterstock.com; page 145: © Torresigner/iStockPhoto.com; page 148: © Hans Geel/Shutterstock.com; page 153: © porosolka/iStockPhoto.com; page 155: © margouillatphotos /iStockPhoto.com; page 158: © DebbiSmirnoff/iStockPhoto.com; page 161: © msheldrake/Shutterstock .com; page 162: © IvanJekic/iStockPhoto.com; page 165: © William C Bunce/Shutterstock.com